Praise for *The Manager's Guide to Preventing a Hostile Work Environment*

"This book is a must-read for executives managing in a business environment, where complex issues such as a perceived hostile workplace can derail even the most successful organization. Leadership needs to understand the public vs. private voice conflict, so well described here. This book provides a practical framework for understanding and managing this challenge."

Robert J. Smith
Regional Executive Officer/Northeast
Willis North America

"Not very long ago, employers found themselves confronted with new risks associated with the ways employees interact with each other. Although the losses that can result from these risks have become well understood, the ways to mitigate the risks have not. Now, managers and supervisors have a roadmap to prevention—in a book that is readable, enlightening, and useful."

Linda Lamel
Former President, The College of Insurance
Former Executive Director, Risk and Insurance
Management Society

"Misunderstood, the challenge of diversity in our workplace can be the spark igniting litigation in virtually any organization. *The Manager's Guide to Preventing a Hostile Work Environment* is a must-read for executives, managers, and employees at any level."

Raphael J. Caprio, Ph.D.
Vice President for Continuous Education and Outreach
Rutgers University

The Manager's Guide to Preventing a Hostile Work Environment

THE MANAGER'S GUIDE TO PREVENTING A HOSTILE WORK ENVIRONMENT

How to Avoid Legal and Financial Risks
By Protecting Your Workplace from
Harassment Based on **Sex, Race,
Disability, Religion,** and **Age**

WANDA DOBRICH, Ph.D.,
STEVEN DRANOFF, Ph.D.
and GERALD MAATMAN, Jr., Esq.

McGraw-Hill

New York   Chicago   San Francisco   Lisbon   London
Madrid   Mexico City   Milan   New Delhi   San Juan
Seoul   Singapore   Sydney   Toronto

McGraw-Hill

A Division of The McGraw·Hill Companies

This book was set in JansonText type by The Composing Room of Michigan, Inc., Grand Rapids, Michigan.

Printed and bound by Quebecor World/Martinsburg.

This publication is designed to provide accurate and authoritative information in regard to the subject matter covered. It is sold with the understanding that neither the author nor the publisher is engaged in rendering legal, accounting, or other professional service. If legal advice or other expert assistance is required, the services of a competent professional person should be sought.
—*From a Declaration of Principles jointly adopted by a Committee of the American Bar Association and a Committee of Publishers.*

This book is printed on recycled, acid-free paper containing a minimum of 50% recycled, de-inked fiber.

Contents

Preface

Managers in the United States operate in a complicated legal environment. Employers and managers face significant legal and financial risks from employee lawsuits. As a result, employment-related claims are escalating, and supervisors often find themselves worried about being sued or accused of wrongdoing for making personnel decisions. Potential legal risks underlie almost all personnel decisions. These problems are no different for small or large companies. Clearly, the potential of being sued for personnel decisions is now an "occupational hazard" for supervisors.

The most significant workplace hazard is exposure for sexual harassment. This book explains how to protect yourself and your organization from the legal and financial risks of sexual harassment as well as other forms of harassment. This is a unique book. It represents a collaborative effort of two industrial psychologists and an employment lawyer, and uses psychology and the law to explain the behaviors that lead to workplace harassment, and how to avoid them.

So why read this book? The reason is simple. It serves as a tool kit to become a better manager, and enables the reader to have a clear understanding of the dangers and proactive remedies for hostile work environment harassment. This type of workplace problem has resulted in multimillion-dollar lawsuits. Whether the hostile environment involves sexual, religious, disability, or age-based harassment, the result is the same—a powder keg of liability for a manager and for an employer.

Discrimination and harassment problems affect businesses of all sizes and shapes. Texaco settled the largest race discrimination class-action case of its kind for $176 million. Publix Supermarkets settled a similar sex discrimination class action for $81.5 million. Large settlements are not reserved for class actions only. Payouts in excess of $1 million are not at all unusual for single claimants. For example, Harvard University was hit for $4 million on *national origin* discrimination, United Airlines for $2.9 million on *religious* discrimination, Seven-Up for $2.5 million on *sexual harassment,* and Merrill Lynch for $1.8 million on *age* discrimination. Each of these cases involved a single employee. Note too that these employers settled *before* going to court, where they would have risked even greater losses.

But money is not all that is at stake for the employer. One recent case amply demonstrates the true scope of the problem. The government sued an employer and various supervisors at a typical white-collar business for alleged hostile work environment sexual harassment. The lawsuit's allegations were that supervisors either participated in sexual banter toward female subordinates or acquiesced in similar conduct by male coworkers of the female employees. The litigation concerned alleged systemic problems of a similar nature throughout the company. After three years of litigation, the company settled the lawsuit for an undisclosed sum in excess of $3 million. Executives and supervisors were distracted from running the business during that entire three-year period, as depositions and discovery in the lawsuit created a situation in which the company was "under siege." Consumers and advocacy groups threatened the company with boycotts, and management suffered through an onslaught of negative publicity. Shareholder activists kept the problem before employees and senior management during annual meetings; the lawsuit and the problems in the company's workplace were the subject of significant discussion in shareholder meetings, watercooler discussions, and employee e-mails. The lesson to be learned from this unfortunate occurrence is that a hostile work environment can create untold problems and liabilities for any company and its management personnel. Fortunately, your organization doesn't have to be the next victim of a debilitating lawsuit. This book explains how to protect yourself and your organization.

Wanda Dobrich
Steven Dranoff
Gerald L. Maatman, Jr.

February 2002

The Manager's Guide to Preventing a Hostile Work Environment

When Hostilities Become Liabilities: Understanding Hostile Work Environment Harassment

WHY ARE WE writing a book for managers about *hostile work environment harassment?*

It is only part of a much larger problem of employment discrimination, which comes in all sizes and shapes in the workplace. From the moment a worker applies for a job to the moment he or she terminates, there are many potential pitfalls of discrimination—subtle and overt—that the proactive manager needs to be aware of. Why single out hostile work environment harassment?

Let's talk for a moment about what hostile work environment harassment *isn't.*

It isn't an employment practice per se, such as hiring, firing, promoting, or compensating workers. When these acts are applied in a way that is biased against particular groups of workers, such as women, older employees, or members of a particular race, it is unlawful. But we are not talking about this kind of discrimination.

We are also not talking about the many ways employers can discriminate against particular groups of workers once they are employed. For instance, employers are not allowed to use biased procedures in evaluating employee performance. They also cannot retaliate against employees who complain of unfair treatment. This type of discrimination may feel "harassing" to its victims, but it is still not *harassment* in a legal sense.

We are not even including in this book any discussion of quid pro quo harassment. This occurs when a supervisor uses his or her authority to wield favors from a subordinate who is a member of a protected class (i.e., sex, race, disability, religion, or age). Conditioning employment benefits on an employee's submission to such requests is illegal, but it is not *hostile work environment harassment*.

All the forms of discrimination we have mentioned so far have one thing in common. They are abuses that occur because a *procedure*—how to hire, how to supervise, how to terminate, etc.—has been violated in its fair application.

Hostile work environment harassment is a different animal. Unlike any other type of employment discrimination, it refers to violations that occur between *people*, not violations in the way people apply *procedures*. It is therefore not quantified in the operating structure of the company. It is not under the employer's direct scrutiny.

Hostile work environment harassment is *interpersonal*.

It is about the way people treat other people while they are working on the job. It is not about how particular groups of people are treated by the employer, but about how individual employees treat other employees because they are members of a particular protected group. It is not about work conditions, but about the conditions people expose others to at work.

Up until the very recent past, the courts left decisions about employee behavior to the discretion of the employer. There have always been some workers who "behave badly." However, this was not illegal discrimination per se, no matter *who* engaged in the suspect behavior or under *what* conditions the behavior occurred. An employee had to demonstrate some tangible loss in employment opportunity or work conditions to make a bona fide claim of employment discrimination.

All this changed with the recent development of law on hostile work environment harassment. For the first time in history, under certain circumstances "bad behavior" can also constitute unlawful behavior. Simply put, when it is directed against a coworker or subordinate on the basis of membership in a protected class, bad behavior is illegal discrimination. Moreover, the hostility is not in the actual behavior itself but in the subjective way it makes victims feel. For example, if a supervisor tells sexually charged jokes during a staff meeting and a female employee is offended by the comments and less able to participate in the rest of meeting as a result of the atmosphere created by the jokes, the bad behavior as perceived by the victim has caused a hostile work environment. The joke teller may not have intended to offend, but the offended female victim nonetheless suffered a violation of legal rights under the new law of hostile work environment harrassment.

Hostile work environment harassment is fuzzy and subjective, which makes it even more dangerous to organizations, and harder to prevent. Perception is turned inside out. Harassment is not measured by the intentions of the harasser or by the bias of the employer. It is measured by the perception of the victim.

Is it a *look*, a *stare*, or a *glare*? Behavior is considered harassing if a "reasonable person" of like characteristics to the member of a protected class would consider it so. Neither employers, nor supervisors, nor employees themselves are fully prepared to deal with this dramatic change in the laws of the workplace.

It used to be that an employer had only to be concerned about its track record in procedural practices. These are easily quantified, and if need be, corrected. Do salaries differ for particular groups? What is the racial breakdown of the work force? Is there a uniform standard to evaluate employee performance? Did the supervisor terminate an employee for refusing a sexual favor? There are objective answers to these questions.

Monitoring the work environment for shifting employee perceptions of harassment is something different. Employers do not even know the questions to ask, much less how to answer them. Whether or not an environment is hostile is subjective. The employer cannot have enough rules to give supervisors to quantify the atmosphere in their departments.

It is therefore not surprising that despite the fact that hostile work environment harassment is just one part of the employment discrimination problem, it is costing employers a disproportionate share of dollars lost to litigation and settlement costs. The number of claims of hostile work environment harassment brought before the U.S. Equal Employment Opportunity Commission (EEOC) for each of the protected classes of employees recognized by federal law increases *every year.*

Employers have been unprepared and unable to bring down these numbers and the huge accompanying liabilities. The reason why is really quite simple. When hostile work environment harassment was first identified as a form of discrimination, the usual remedies were applied. Employers redrafted policies to include it, and employee training was extended to cover it.

The problem was, the usual remedies failed to take into account that hostile work environment harassment differed from earlier recognized forms of employment discrimination in all the significant ways we just outlined. Traditional approaches in teaching employees the dos and don'ts worked well for procedural types of discrimination, but not for hostile work environment harassment. This is because human behavior is not reducible to yes and no judgments. Intentions are even harder to prove. And how coworkers will react to one another is unpredictable.

There are no procedural remedies that can correct employees' (mis)perceptions, which are so often the cause of a claim of hostile work environment harassment. Employees interpret interactions based on their personal history and what perceptions they bring to the table.

The Public and the Private Voice

We are sympathetic to the wish for easy "rules" by which to avoid hostile work environment harassment. From much research, however, we know that when employees make judgments about workplace hostility, they use information that is above and below their horizon of awareness. We call these zones the *public* and *private* voice, respectively. To prevent hostile work environment harassment, we believe managers and supervisors need to understand the difference between employees' private voices and their public ones.

The public voice is the socially correct way we have learned to treat people. The corporation's antiharassment policy echoes its public voice. When a male employee says that he would never refer to a woman using derogatory or sexualized language, he is expressing his public voice.

The public voice is in our zone of awareness. It is based on how we have been raised—the values we have been taught in school and in the community—and it summarizes our beliefs. Because the public voice is a conscious part of us, we can modify it as we absorb new information over the course of life.

But this is not all that motivates workplace perception.

Employees also have a private voice. It consists of our personal impressions of people and events that are also gathered over a lifetime of experience. If the public voice is what we *think* we should feel, the private voice is what we *really* think and feel. Unlike the public voice, however, which can be heard by others, the private voice is inaudible. Sometimes even we ourselves are unaware of it.

Yet as psychologists (and as a lawyer who has tried lawsuits in front of juries), we know that the private voice strongly influences the way we act. Because it is not always accessible, it affects us in ways that we neither are immediately aware of nor have control over. For example, when an employee "slips" and tells an off-color joke that offends a coworker, this may be the work of the private voice.

When the public and private voice are in agreement—that is, we *think* and *feel* the same way about something—our actions will be consistent and clear. In the case of hostile work environment harassment, if the public voice of the corporation policy is in agreement with an employee's private voice, the risk of engaging or becoming embroiled in harassment is low.

If, on the other hand, the public and private perceptions of an employee are *not* in alignment, the risk of hostile work environment harassment increases dramatically. This is true for victims and harassers alike. Even when an employee tries to "do the right thing" and follows the dictates of the public voice, if inner perceptions pull in another direction, the private voice will inevitably surface in one way or another in behavior that creates a hostile work environment. Misalignment of public and private voices in the victim and the harasser is the fertile ground from which most hostile work environment lawsuits grow.

As we look at each of the protected categories of employees in this book, we will see that the public and private voices can be in different stages of evolution. For example, a public voice can be "overlearned" or "undereducated." For many of the older protected categories, employees have already deeply internalized the public voice. Race is a good example. It is hard to imagine an American worker today who does not know that racial slurring or name-calling is wrong.

Though equally protected under the umbrella of Title VII law, members of other protected classes do not receive the same benefits of a strong public voice. Some examples are certain psychiatric or learning disorders. Coworkers may not be as empathic to these individuals because they do not think even *publicly* that they are deserving of special consideration. Sometimes reeducation of the public voice, such as in AIDS awareness, helps reduce hostile work environment harassment for targeted members of these groups.

The relationship between the public and the private voice is complex. In some cases of hostile work environment harassment, the harasser's public voice "knows better," but the private voice intrudes anyway. The harasser may or may not be aware of the misalignment. In other cases, the harasser's public voice is undereducated, and so it does not exert the necessary control over the private voice. In this case, the harasser feels self-righteous about the harassment conduct.

The victim's public and private voices are also in conflict when hostile environment work harassment occurs. Sometimes the victim's public voice believes the mistreatment is wrong, but the private voice feels it is deserved. In other cases, the victim's public voice is uncertain of where the ground lies, but the private voice reacts strongly.

In any event, the public and private voices of the victim and/or the harasser are always in misalignment. When only one of the parties is in conflict however, it is unlikely the harassment will go on for very long. We know of many employees who are subjected to hostile work environment harassment and are able to effectively stop it before it escalates or gets out of control. But this may still not end the harassment problem for the employer, because the harasser in this case most often moves on to another target who is less able to protect himself or herself.

When *both* the harasser and the victim are in misalignment, the problem is much more serious. A tag team of public and private voices wrestles on the workplace mat. While the public voices of the employees argue about the literal "facts of the matter," the private voices wage the real fight, below the surface of conscious awareness. Neither protagonist hears his or her or the opponent's private voice, and the battle rages without stop. These are the cases that eventually fall into the lap of the jury—12 men and women who are asked to make reasonable judgments based on partial information.

We use this as a very simple formula throughout this book:

The risk of hostile work environment harassment increases dramatically when the public and private voices of both the harasser and victim are in misalignment.

The manager's task is to prevent a potentially dangerous hostile work environment claim by working with the harasser and victim to realign critical misperceptions so that the conflicts that are fueling the harassment crisis abate. For example, using the case of the off-color joke, assume that the employee who "slips" tells a derogatory joke that is demeaning to women. Let us assume further that he is really angry with the woman coworker who "overhears" the joke because she won an account or gained a work benefit he thinks he deserved. If the manager addresses only the employee's joke-telling behavior (his public voice), will this end the problem?

Not a chance!

This employee's resentment will resurface in another form. Suppose, on the other hand, the manager inquires of the employee what prompted him to tell the joke. Is there a concern that hides behind the "humor"? Now the supervisor has a good shot at learning the true motivation of the harassment act and can be in a position to take steps to correct the real problem. Will this reduce the likelihood of another joke?

You bet!

The proactive supervisor does not stop here. It is also important to consider the private voice of the accuser. In the hypothetical case, she may be entirely innocent in the matter of the off-color joke. Alternatively, there may be some truth to the joke teller's claim of "injustice" that the supervisor was not aware of. Again, correcting the real problem is the best prevention against continuing harassment.

In exploring the private voices of *both* parties, the proactive supervisor gets a heads-up on potential molehills before they become mountains. Seen in this light, hostile work environment harassment is a symptom of a larger problem between employees in the department. Harassment symptoms are signals: They are yellow lights to alert supervisors to potential danger. Supervisors are ill-advised to ignore them.

There is one caveat to this.

The manager can also be in misalignment. Supervisors, like other employees, have public and private voices. The harassment schism deepens if managers too are pulled asunder by the dictates of a misaligned public and private voice. This disables the realigning of the victim and harasser through the supervision process.

Finally, misalignment can also occur between the public and private voices of the employer. Some organizations have procedural safeguards against discrimination and harassment, but passively fail to enforce them. In this case, a strong public voice hides a disingenuous private voice. This derails the manager and trickles down to the level of the individual employee, creating a dangerous legal environment.

In other cases, though this is less frequent today, the organization may lack a formal antiharassment policy and complaint procedure. This is a case of an organization with a deficient public voice. Such a company cannot hope to systematically protect its employees from discrimination.

Supervisors play the most critical role in correcting the misalignments that occur throughout a hostile work environment harassment scenario. They are in a dangerous position, intermediaries between executive management, who make the policies, and employees, who are embroiled in the harassment problem. If the supervisors fail to address a known harassment problem between employees (even employees they do not supervise), they expose themselves and the employer to risk. In some states, supervisors are personally liable in harassment cases. In all states, however, company policies require that supervisors report known harassment to assigned agents in the corporation; failure to do so can result in termination.

Supervisors are therefore "translators" of the public and private voice up and down the highway of communication, zigzagging across layers of the organization. They must make sure critical misalignments are corrected so that all parties pull together on the same team, must know what others are thinking, and must be able to use the information constructively to end the harassment problem in the department. Clearly, supervisors are on the front line of the legal battlefield, for employers will suffer liability in this context if supervisory personnel fail to live up to their responsibilities.

Notice that we say the harassment *problem*. It is, of course, not the job of the supervisor to make a decision about the legitimacy of a harassment *complaint*. Human resources (or another assigned agent) formally investigates hostile work environment harassment. Unless explicitly instructed otherwise, most managers have no direct input into the formal resolution.

Most workers who are accused of hostile work environment harassment, however, are not summarily terminated from the organization. The job of supervising victims and harassers after an incident has been reported falls to the department manager. Life goes on, and the employee conflicts that fuel a harassment complaint do not end with the investigation, at least in most cases.

Throughout this book, therefore, we distinguish between the harassment *complaint* and the harassment *problem*. Executive management monitors the former, but supervisors monitor the latter. Human resources oversees the *procedural* aspects of the harassment, whereas managers oversee the *interpersonal* aspects. It is a complicated matrix of overlapping responsibilities.

Once human resources has intervened, the proactive manager does not hide his or her head in the sand and think that the problem is over. In actual practice, the organization is at greatest risk for continued problems *after* harassment has been reported and investigated.

Opening Pandora's Box

We now offer a full answer to the question posed at the beginning of this chapter. Why are we writing a book specifically for managers, covering *only* the topic of hostile work environment harassment?

Managers have the most critical role in the corporation to prevent hostile work environment harassment but are given the least formal training to do it.

From our experiences in counseling employers and consulting with corporations across the United States, we learned that no one systematically prepares managers for this special job. Just as uncomfortable with workplace harassment as anyone else, managers have little guidance on how to supervise employees who either accuse a coworker or are themselves accused of hostile work environment harassment.

Seven Steps to Realignment

We offer the manager seven steps to help realign the public and private voices of all parties involved in a hostile work environment harassment problem. We will go through these steps for the five protected categories of employees that have the highest rates of reported complaints.

In the first step, the misalignment is between the public and private voices of the victim. A harassment victim almost always knows the right thing to say or do to address a hostile work environment problem, but something stops the person from doing it. How can the manager help this employee remove the roadblocks and regain confidence as a productive worker in the department?

In the second step, the misalignment is between the public and private voices of the harasser. Managers typically find this employee the most difficult to supervise. The sources of misalignment can be many. The biggest issue is rehabilitation potential. Will the harasser get into trouble again? How can the manager reduce risk to other employees in the department but still protect the rights of the accused? What is the manager's obligation to the employer, in terms of both upholding the norms of appropriate conduct and promoting a culture of respect in the workplace? The manager or supervisor must monitor the work atmosphere in the department and be responsible for recognizing and acting on employee problems as they arise.

Supervisors are employees, too. Just as harassers and victims can have misalignments of their public and private voices, so can managers. In the third and fourth steps, we show how this can affect the capacity of managers to be empathic when supervising harassers and victims. When empathy is lost, or when managers take sides, they are less able to help these employees explore their perceptions and misperceptions about the issues at work that give rise to the harassment problem.

The potential for misalignment continues. So far, we have moved through two layers of the organization, the harassment parties and their direct supervisors. A hostile environment harassment problem has still greater reach. The employer also has a public and private voice. How the company responds to all these parties, including the supervisor, has bearing on the harassment outcome and future prevention.

When the corporation is misaligned, the antiharassment policy does little good to the victim or the harasser. Managers play an important role in bringing the private voices of the victim and the harasser to the attention of the employer.

While managers do not have control over the corporation's responses to them, many employers are willing and able to make important changes when supervisors bring such misalignments to their attention. When the employer is not, supervisors need to consider ways to protect themselves from getting caught in the middle. In the fifth and sixth steps, we describe how managers advocate for victims, give employers needed information to make decisions about the safety of all workers in the department, and protect themselves.

The seventh and final step addresses the misalignment of coworkers. Employee training is the vehicle to open discussion on the perception of other workers in the department. Hostile work environment harassment is a "family affair." It is not an accident that it has earned its name—hostile work *environment* harassment. It is a malady that infects the work atmosphere, which by definition extends beyond the particular employees who are directly involved. It is a safe bet that when hostile work environment harassment occurs, it is symptomatic of other subtle (or not so subtle) employee problems that affect the whole department. Training is a vehicle to explore coworker perceptions, and it is especially important in companies in which hostile work environment harassment has already occurred. We describe in each chapter the kind of training that is helpful to mobilize coworkers to their best potential.

Preventing hostile work environment harassment always requires more than a correction of the harassment *complaint*. It requires a positive change in the environment of the department in which the harassment *problem* occurred. Training helps the manager reinforce consensus on a uniform public and private voice, which brings the workplace culture into alignment with the law.

How to Use This Book

This book is a primer on preventing hostile work environment harassment. It is written especially for supervisors and focuses on each of the five major categories in which employees are protected from harassment by federal law under

Title VII—sex, race, disability, religion, and age. The book can be used as a reference if the supervisor has a particular employee problem, or it can be read in its entirety as a guide to preventing a hostile work environment from developing in the first place.

Before presenting the protected categories, we offer, in Chapter 2, a blueprint of the laws on hostile work environment harassment. This discussion is general and applies to employees who fall under any of the protected categories. While it is not intended as legal advice for a particular case, our goal is to familiarize the manager with the universal concepts that govern the supervision of all employees. We advise reading Chapter 2 before reviewing any of the subsequent chapters on particular types of hostile work environment harassment. In each of the chapters, we include an overview of the particular issues the specific category highlights, case vignettes, and a discussion of the seven steps.

The harassers and victims in the examples we use throughout this book represent a spectrum of misalignment. Some have need of a stronger public voice, others need clarification of their private voices, and so on. For the manager, what is most important to focus on is how the seven-step process is applied, regardless of the particulars of the case.

What Every Manager Needs to Know about the Laws of the Workplace

The Challenge

M ANAGERS ARE responsible for abiding by workplace laws on a day-to-day basis and making sure their employees do the same. Ignorance of these laws is not a defense to a worker's lawsuit. An ill-informed or uninformed executive risks exposing his or her business to significant financial and legal liability by failing to stay up to date on workplace law— or failing to conscientiously observe it.

Employment-related litigation has reached epidemic proportions in the United States. Such claims have increased at a phenomenal rate. By 2000, the backlog of charges filed with the EEOC and analogous state agencies reached their highest levels ever (at the federal level, over 100,000 charges). In the period 1990–2000, employment discrimination claims filed with the federal government increased by double-digit percentages each year, and the backlog of discrimination charges awaiting resolution more than doubled. At the same time, workplace discrimination lawsuits are now estimated to represent more than one-fifth of the nearly 250,000 federal civil lawsuits filed in the United States.

Against this backdrop, the Internet revolution has changed the landscape of employer-employee relations. Lawyers representing workers maintain Web sites with downloadable documents on workplace rights and strategies for suing employers. Employees, ex-employees, or third parties post complaints about employers, their personnel policies and benefits packages, and even individual personnel decisions on Yahoo message boards. Worse still, an increasingly destructive tactic has been the creation of Web pages by ex-employees devoted to employee-initiated litigation against a company; these Web pages collect and catalog workplace complaints, and often invite the viewer to download more information on joining the lawsuits as a suing party. Not to be outdone, other Web sites invite postings about "the boss from hell" or "the worst employer on earth," and provide links to do-it-yourself kits on how to "sue the company" or "keep your boss in line."

In this climate, it is not uncommon for discharged workers to sue their former employer or supervisor simply out of a feeling that they were treated harshly or unfairly. Sometimes the lawsuit is for the purpose of getting back at their ex-employer or former boss. Such claims impose significant costs and expenses on employers. In turn, executives and supervisors spend enormous amounts of time, energy, and money in the defense of employment-related litigation. In recognition of this environment of litigiousness, over 100 insurance companies in the United States now offer coverage for employment practices liability insurance.

The greatest number of workplace legal claims over the past decade are those alleging harassment—primarily sexual harassment, but also harassment based on other legally impermissible grounds such as race, age, religion, or disability. Over 1 million claims have been filed. This suggests that one of the principal challenges of supervisors is to provide an environment where respect and dignity are accorded to all employees. This is the most basic form of preventing workplace harassment.

This book seeks to arm and empower managers and supervisors to identify and avoid the legal and financial risks caused by workplace harassment. Knowledge of these dangers and risks, along with strategies to minimize or avoid them, is essential to managers. Increased productivity, corporate reputation, and fiscal responsibility are directly related to and impacted by the prevention of lawsuits alleging harassment. Creating the best possible employer-employee relations also enables an employer to have a competitive edge. Indeed, since employees are often a company's most valuable resource, managing employee relations is at the heart of an executive's responsibilities.

This book attempts to explain laws of the workplace relating to harassment. The goal is to help managers understand potential liabilities and then identify, avoid, and manage them. By using the suggested effective human resource practices and training strategies in this book, managers will be able to maximize workplace productivity and lessen or minimize potential liabilities for harassment problems.

If executives and supervisors are sensitized to the situations that breed employment-related claims, then lawsuits can be avoided or their likelihood can be reduced. Practical and effective management strategies also encourage the early identification and prompt resolution of any harassment problems while creating a workplace characterized by trust, fairness, and good employee relations. When and if lawsuits do arise, the same management strategies and decision-making protocols are designed to enable employers to assert the best possible defenses against any such claims, thereby making the lawsuits easier (and cheaper) to defend.

Legal Liabilities in the Workplace

An Overview of Workplace Law

There is no "one" workplace law in the United States. A patchwork quilt of federal, state, and local laws grants various rights and protections to workers. These laws also impose a multitude of obligations and responsibilities upon managers.

U.S. employment laws impact all personnel decisions made by business executives. These laws provide rights and protections to workers from the start of the application process to the end of their work for a company, whether they've been fired, have resigned, or have retired. In this respect, the laws cover workers from cradle to grave.

As a practical matter, the greatest number of employment-related claims comes from employees who have been fired and workplace harassment problems. To avoid such claims business executives and supervisors must have an appreciation for the laws that apply to the workplace.

The At-Will Employment Rule in Theory

Although the United States has numerous worker protection laws, employees generally have relatively limited legal rights when compared with those in many other developed nations. The primary reason for this is a legal concept known as the *at-will employment rule*. This rule of law evolved in the late 1800s when workers "sold" their skills and labor to the highest bidder and moved freely from job to job; likewise, employers could freely hire and fire workers.

In theory, the at-will employment rule of law provides that just as a worker without an employment contract is free to quit his or her job at any time, a business executive or supervisor may fire an employee for any reason, without notice, and at any time. The termination can be made without any financial obligation whatsoever to the discharged worker. In essence, an employee works at the will and whim of the employer.

In theory, a manager may terminate an at-will employee (i.e., an employee without a contract) without legal risk. For example, a firing decision based on any of the following factors would be legal in the case of an at-will employee:

- "I don't like your attitude."
- "Things aren't working out."
- "I've changed my mind about needing your services."

In theory, courts would rule that so long as there is no agreement between the employer and the employee for a fixed term of employment, an employer could terminate the worker for any of these reasons. One can reasonably suggest that these results are unfair, but there is no law requiring workplace fairness. As a result, an at-will worker who is fired by an employer would be unable to bring a viable legal claim over termination.

Significantly, the at-will employment rule does not require an employer to develop an employee handbook, a bonus program, or a training curriculum on avoiding harassment. In general, employers can develop and enforce any reasonable workplace policies at their own discretion. The law and the courts grant great leeway and discretion to employers to administer their workplace policies as they deem appropriate.

The At-Will Employment Rule in Practice

The at-will employment rule is a creature of state law. The main compliance problem for employers is that the rule is not interpreted uniformly in all 50 states. Some jurisdictions interpret the rule broadly, whereas courts in other states have created exceptions to the rule or otherwise restrict the application of the at-will employment doctrine.

One thing is clear—the trend of courts in the past decade has been to grant additional rights to workers, and thus the at-will employment rule is being interpreted much more narrowly. As a result, "wrongful termination" litigation is a fact of life for employers in America. Prudent business executives and supervisors must recognize that exceptions to the at-will employment rule have steadily eroded the doctrine to the point that managers face significant legal restrictions on their ability to fire employees and defend harassment litigation. The days of "risk-free" personnel decisions are long gone in the United States.

More importantly, executives who wish to avoid legal claims must be mindful of the practical realities of the at-will employment rule when they manage their employees. At-will employees who are fired often sue their employers. Employers necessarily incur costs in defending such lawsuits. The participation of executives and supervisors in the defense of these cases inevitably drains away valuable time better spent on running the business and managing the work force. Firing decisions—especially when responding to harassment complaints—must take account of these practicalities.

Federal and State Employment Discrimination Laws

The most important exceptions to the at-will employment rule are contained in key federal and state laws prohibiting employment discrimination. Laws enacted by the U.S. Congress are known as *federal statutory laws*. As such, federal statutory laws apply throughout the United States. In contrast, the 50 states also have sets of statutory laws, which are termed *state statutory laws*. The statutory laws of a state generally apply only to activity taking place or having an effect on persons within the state.

Federal statutory law prohibits discrimination against workers based upon age, sex, national origin, race, color, religion, disability, and pregnancy. The majority of these prohibitions are found in a law that is commonly referred to as *Title VII of the Civil Rights Act of 1964* (Title VII). The *Pregnancy Discrimination Act of 1978* (PDA) prohibits discrimination based on pregnancy. Age discrimination is prohibited by a separate law called the *Age Discrimination in Employment Act of 1967* (ADEA). The *Americans with Disabilities Act* (ADA) prohibits discrimination based on a disability. Finally, the *Civil Rights Act of 1991* establishes damage remedies for victims of illegal conduct, implements Title VII, the PDA, the ADEA, and the ADA, and clarifies various issues under these laws.

Harassment is a form of discrimination. If an employer harasses an employee due to the employee's membership in any of the protected categories above, the employer is deemed by law to have committed an act of employment discrimination. Some state employment discrimination statutes prohibit the same kinds of harassment outright. Federal employment discrimination laws and other state statutes have been interpreted by federal and state courts to prohibit harassment as a form of illegal discrimination. The result is the same—employees who suffer harassment due to their membership in a protected category have legal rights and are protected by law.

Federal statutory laws banning employment discrimination are exceedingly broad in scope and protect all types of workers—those who have individual employment contracts, those who are employed at will, and even those covered by collective bargaining agreements. These laws also protect job applicants from discrimination in the hiring process, as well as ex-employees and even retirees in certain circumstances. Most significantly, these laws also prohibit any form of retaliation against employees who assert any complaint of discrimination or who support another worker in a complaint of discrimination.

Executives and supervisors are not required to hire or promote individuals protected by these laws or to favor such individuals over others. In addition, employers are not required to lower their standards or expectations for such employees. Rather, employment discrimination laws simply prohibit employers from taking an individual's membership in a protected category into consideration in their treatment of workers or in making any employment-related decision.

> **There is a very narrow exception to federal employment discrimination laws called a *bona fide occupational qualification* (BFOQ). This limited exception provides that if, for example, a particular sex, religion, or national origin is necessary to the performance of a job (i.e., it is a BFOQ for the job), an employer may discriminate against an applicant or employee who is not of that sex, religion, or national origin for the purpose of the job in question. A successful BFOQ defense is recognized by courts only in rare circumstances. For example, a health club operator can impose a male-only job requirement consistent with the law for the job of locker room attendant in the men's locker room of the health club if that job requires the employee to be present in the shower facilities of the locker room.**

Title VII, the PDA, the ADEA, the ADA, and the Civil Rights Act of 1991 apply to all terms and conditions of employment—from the time of hiring to an employee's termination or retirement and virtually all aspects of employment in between. These federal statutes also apply to all but the smallest employers, as only business entities with fewer than 15 workers in the United States are generally exempt from these laws. The ADEA has a slightly higher threshold for coverage; it applies to companies having 20 or more workers in the United States.

All but 2 of the 50 states (Georgia and Mississippi being the exceptions) have comprehensive statutory laws prohibiting employment discrimination by private employers. These state statutory laws generally mirror the federal employment discrimination laws. However, some states actually provide greater protections than Title VII, the PDA, the ADEA, the ADA, and the Civil Rights Act of 1991. Examples of state statutory laws that are broader than federal law include those that prohibit discrimination on the basis of marital status, sexual orientation, or genetic traits. These state statutory laws also generally apply to smaller employers who are otherwise exempt from federal employment discrimination laws (e.g., any employer with more than 1 but fewer than 15 employees). In addition, many local governments have enacted ordinances prohibiting discrimination. Therefore, in major metropolitan areas in the United States, it is not uncommon for three sets of laws—federal, state, and local—to prohibit employment discrimination.

Individuals covered by these laws are termed *protected-category employees.*

Protected-Category Employees

Individuals covered by federal, state, and local employment discrimination laws are known as protected-category employees. The major protected categories include:

• Age	• Religion
• Color	• Sex
• Disability	• Sexual orientation
• National origin	• Veteran status
• Pregnancy	• Race

Some believe that the only ones not protected by law are white males under 40 years of age (WMUFs), but this is a myth, since such individuals may well be protected-category employees due to sex (e.g., an employer may not discriminate against men by favoring women), or on account of their religion, national origin, veteran status, or the existence of a disability. Likewise, an employer may not discriminate against WMUFs by favoring African-American workers (known as *reverse discrimination*) or retaliate against WMUFs for supporting others who complain about alleged workplace discrimination. In this respect, federal, state, and local employment discrimination laws swallow up the at-will employment rule.

Common Law Doctrines Bearing upon Employment

Quite apart from federal, state, and local employment discrimination laws, many states have recognized additional exceptions to the at-will employment rule through judicial decisions. In the U.S. legal system, judicial decisions create what is called *common law*. It is a body of law based on prior legal rulings or precedents rather than statutes. In the employment context, business executives and supervisors must be mindful of both common law *tort* and *contract* theories.

A *tort* is the legal term for what is known as a private wrong caused by behavior that is inconsistent with that of a reasonable person. For example, a person who causes an automobile accident by traveling too fast for road conditions has committed a tort. In the employment law context, an executive who deviates from common law rules in the workplace can be subject to tort liability from workers injured by the executive's conduct. Employment-related claims are often brought under state common law concepts based on a host of tort theories. By asserting these claims, employees can seek damages in excess of those available in lawsuits claiming breach of employment contracts. Tort claims are most commonly asserted in cases of alleged workplace harassment.

Tort claims can be based on several different legal theories. For example, workers frequently resort to the tort of *defamation* based on the allegation that an executive or supervisor has made false statements about the worker to other employees, third parties, or potential employers. Common law defamation claims are established if an employee can prove that the executive or supervisor intentionally made a false statement about the worker, the statement was made to a third party, and the statement caused injury to the worker. A defamatory statement made orally is termed *slander*. If the statement is written, the claim is one for *libel*. Defamation actions can arise in a broad range of employment-related situations. Typically, most claims stem from statements made in the context of charges of harassment or statements made in providing postemployment references. While defenses to a defamation action vary under the common law of most states, truth is always a complete defense. Many states also recognize either an *absolute privilege* or *qualified privilege* in statements made by executives or supervisors about workers if the executive or supervisor had a duty to speak or write about the employee's termination (such as, for example, advising a state unemployment compensation agency as to the reason for the worker's termination). The privilege is upheld if the statement was made in good faith and was disseminated only to those employees within the company who had a need to know the information.

Another tort claim alleged frequently by employees is the theory of *intentional infliction of emotional distress*. To establish such a claim, the employee must demonstrate that the executive or supervisor engaged in extreme and outrageous conduct. Most jurisdictions define this as conduct that is so outrageous in character and extreme in degree as to go beyond all possible bounds of decency. The termination of an employee, in and of itself, generally does not establish intentional inflicted emotional distress. An executive or supervisor must commit some egregious act above and beyond firing the employee, such as physically restraining the employee during an investigatory interview. Severe acts of harassment generally give rise to a situation in which such claims are asserted.

Fraud and *misrepresentation* are also alleged by an increasing number of workers. To establish fraud or misrepresentation, an employee must prove that the executive or supervisor made an actual representation of a material fact with knowledge of its falsity or with reckless disregard for the truth. In the employment context, most fraud claims are brought after terminations and are based on promises about specific benefits or bonuses that were to be paid or with respect to the permanency or stability of the worker's employment.

The tort claim of *invasion of privacy* is also frequently asserted by workers. The common law of a growing number of states recognizes that an employee has a common law right of privacy into which an employer cannot unreasonably interfere. These types of claims are often brought in the context of harassment situations. For example, where a supervisor has questioned an employee about his or her sexual practices and made suggestive comments about such proclivities, lawyers sometimes also assert *breach of privacy* claims because of the unreasonable nature of the questions to the employee about such private matters.

Finally, *assault* and *battery* are separate intentional torts that are often included as separate claims in harassment cases. An assault occurs if there is an attempt to inflict physical injury. A battery occurs when the assault is accomplished. Victims of harassment frequently bring common law tort claims for assault and battery along with statutory discrimination claims.

Personal Legal Liability of Managers and Supervisors

Managers must realize that violation of many of these federal and state laws may result in their own *personal legal liability*, quite apart from the potential liability of their employer. Some federal courts have imposed personal legal liability upon individual supervisors and executives for acts of discrimination or retaliation against employees. Lawsuits alleging violations of federal employment laws are filed in federal trial courts, which are called *U.S. District Courts.* These courts issue decisions interpreting federal statutory law, which in turn are reviewed by appellate courts upon the request of a party; the appellate courts are known as *U.S. Courts of Appeal,* of which there are 12 in various major cities in the United States. At the current time, federal district courts and appellate courts have issued conflicting opinions about whether individual supervisors and executives can be held personally liable for damages in a lawsuit alleging violations of federal employment discrimination laws. The issue ultimately will be decided by the *U.S. Supreme Court,* the highest court in America. Until such time as the U.S. Supreme Court might interpret the Civil Rights Act of 1991 to prohibit damage recoveries against executives and supervisors in their individual capacity, management personnel will continue to face potential personal legal exposure under federal statutory laws for acts of employment discrimination or retaliation.

More importantly, separate and apart from the question of potential personal legal liability under federal law, many state and local laws impose such liability upon managers, especially for common law tort claims. Managers are often sued for hundreds of thousands of dollars in these types of cases. As a result, a conflict of interest may arise in the legal defense of the employer and the manager. This may require the retention of a separate attorney to defend the manager, thereby increasing the overall costs of the litigation. While employers generally are required to pay for a manager's attorney's fees, in an adverse court judgment, or a settlement involving compensatory damages, many employers will not compensate managers for punitive damages or are prohibited from doing so on account of state corporation laws. Thus, a manager's compliance with these laws is more than a matter of professionalism. It is also a matter of personal financial interest.

Potential Criminal Law Liability for Workplace Problems

In several countries (most notably, Brazil, France, Italy, and Russia), managers can be prosecuted under criminal laws for harassment or certain prohibited acts in making personnel decisions. Generally speaking, executives in the United States do not face criminal prosecution under federal or state law for personnel decisions or harassment—the only liability is under *civil* laws. However, the city of Cleveland, Ohio, enacted a municipal ordinance in 1996 that makes employment discrimination an illegal criminal act. Management personnel can be liable personally under the ordinance; the penalties can include either six months in jail, a fine of up to $5,000, or both. The Cleveland ordinance has been the focus of intense scrutiny by municipal governments throughout the United States. It remains to be seen whether criminalizing employment discrimination becomes a legislative trend in the future.

Quite apart from employment discrimination laws, executives and supervisors often face criminal assault and battery charges in sexual harassment situations involving inappropriate touching. This occurs when the alleged victim makes a criminal complaint against the alleged harasser, who then must defend himself or herself in a criminal trial brought by a local or county prosecutor. Imprisonment and fines are possible, and a guilty verdict can make the defense of a sexual harassment claim virtually impossible in a subsequent civil lawsuit.

Potential Legal Exposure from Employment-Related Lawsuits

Employment-related litigation can be very expensive. These legal exposures have several aspects. An executive or employer sued by an ex-employee faces an incredible financial burden. Employment discrimination cases under federal, state, and local statutory laws are particularly expensive. In this type of litigation, an employee who wins his or her case can recover an award equivalent to lost salary, fringe benefits, *compensatory damages*, and *punitive damages*. Compensatory damages are for the alleged pain, suffering, and emotional distress experienced by the employee injured by the employer's discriminatory conduct or other wrongful acts. Punitive damages are more in the form of a penalty and are imposed to deter wrongful conduct or to punish a lawbreaker. Current federal employment discrimination laws limit awards of compensatory and punitive damages up to $300,000 for most large employers of 500 or more employees; damages are capped at lesser amounts based on a sliding scale of employee populations for smaller companies. However, state and local laws prohibiting employment discrimination generally have no limits on the size of compensatory or punitive damage awards available to employees or ex-employees suing their employer or supervisor. As a result, employers have experienced multimillion-dollar jury verdicts being awarded to employees for state or local law claims over the last decade.

Employees who win employment discrimination cases are also entitled to *prejudgment interest* on the monetary award rendered by the court in his or her favor. By law, interest generally runs from the date of the employee's injury and is calculated at the prime rate and compounded daily. For that reason it is not uncommon for an employment-related lawsuit to present damages of several hundred thousand dollars.

The message should be clear: If you are sued, you lose. This is because even if a company eventually wins the lawsuit on the merits, employers and their management personnel also face the monetary loss attributable to the time spent in defending the case and working with their own lawyers in responding to the litigation. Often this will consume many hours of a manager's time and detract the manager's attention from running the business. Likewise, it is not unusual for executives and supervisors named in a lawsuit to experience morale problems, both their own as well their subordinates'. These factors also represent a loss in productivity and a drain on the employer's human resources.

Finally, an employee's lawsuit incurs costs just to defend the claim. The attorney's fees for the lawyers defending the employer can be significant. These costs are even greater if a conflict of interest exists between the employer and a manager named in the lawsuit, and necessitates the retention of a separate attorney to defend the manager. Defense fees can exceed $250,000 in complex termination or harassment cases, particularly in cases that go to trial.

Heightened Exposure for Attorney's Fees in Employment Litigation

Employment-related litigation is also very expensive because of a special rule regarding attorney's fees. In the American legal system, the person bringing a lawsuit is called the *plaintiff*. The person or entity being sued is called the *defendant*. In most types of legal actions in the United States, the plaintiff pays his or her own attorney's fees. This is known as the English rule of attorney's fees, as it is based on centuries-old court rules and procedures in England. This arrangement is thought to work as an incentive to keep small, unimportant, or questionable matters out of the court system.

Employment-related litigation is different. *Federal, state, and local employment discrimination laws generally require an employer to pay the attorney's fees of the employee in addition to the fees of its own lawyer.* The English rule does not apply. Federal, state, and local employment discrimination laws have special provisions that provide that a plaintiff who wins his or her case is also entitled to an award of attorney's fees. So in any employment discrimination case where an employee brings a case and is successful in proving the claim, the court will award money to the plaintiff to compensate the plaintiff not only for damages but also for attorney's fees.

The U.S. Congress and state legislatures enacted this special attorney's fees rule based on the notion that the purposes of employment discrimination laws would be served by vigorous enforcement of the laws. This purpose is furthered by making it easy for plaintiffs to sue, imposing attorney's fees on employers, and promoting a system where attorneys will have an economic incentive to represent workers. Attorney's fees in this context are set by market rates. This means that in most major metropolitan areas, an award of attorney's fees can be quite substantial. In a complex termination or harassment case, it is not uncommon for the plaintiff's lawyer to request an award of over $100,000 in attorney's fees.

This attorney's fees rule has two practical effects. First, it increases the potential financial exposure and cost of all employment-related litigation. Because the attorney representing the employee in a discrimination case knows that his or her fees ultimately will be paid by the employer (assuming, of course, some modicum of success in the case), the plaintiff's attorney has an economic incentive to put a lot of time and effort into the litigation. This drives up the potential damages of the case, since each hour the employee's attorney spends on the case adds to its value for the plaintiff (and adds to the potential damages faced by the employer). Second, it encourages more cases to be brought, even arguably unmeritorious ones that might otherwise have never been brought forward. Some plaintiffs' attorneys try to use the potential liability for attorney's fees to force employers to offer settlements even for questionable claims. For instance, some employers would rather settle a weak claim for $5,000 than to spend $20,000 in attorney's fees defending the claim. Likewise, an employer often may not wish to risk a trial since the potential damages will include a significant sum for the fees of the plaintiff's attorney. In many cases it is not uncommon for the fees of the employee's attorney to exceed the value of the employee's damages attributable to losing a job or experiencing harassment. Thus, settlement values often correlate to the time and effort of the plaintiff's attorney in prosecuting the case.

Conversely, a frustrating fact of the American legal system for employers and business executives is that a plaintiff does not have to pay the attorney's fees of the defendant where the plaintiff loses his or her case. In essence, the plaintiff has everything to gain and nothing to lose. Admittedly, the law provides that a plaintiff may be required to pay the attorney's fees of a defendant in the narrow circumstance where the plaintiff prosecuted an obviously frivolous case. However, for all practical purposes, judges generally are hesitant to rule in favor of defendants and against plaintiffs on this issue, and awards of attorney's fees to employers are exceedingly rare.

The bottom line for employers is clear. Litigation over personnel decisions and workplace harassment is time-consuming and inconsistent with keeping a clear focus on running a business. It is also the most expensive type of litigation a company will ever battle. The manager's challenge then is to prevent workplace harassment from ever happening in the first place.

Understanding Sexual Harassment Law: The Most Common (and Most Costly) Form of Harassment

ALTHOUGH ALL TYPES of harassment claims are increasing in number, sexual harassment claims are the most prevalent and have received the most media attention. Sexual harassment exposures are also the most prevalent, for women make up a large percentage of the work force as compared to other protected-category groups. Human nature being what it is, people are particularly adept at interacting in ways that create the potential for sexual harassment problems.

Hostile environment sexual harassment is therefore a good test case for managers to use to learn about the laws of the workplace. The legal issues this kind of harassment raises are similar to those brought before the courts for all other types of harassment cases that apply to employees in any of the protected categories.

The subject of sexual harassment became focused in the spotlight of national attention in November 1991 during the confirmation hearing before the U.S. Senate on the nomination of Clarence Thomas for justice of the U.S. Supreme Court. Ironically, Thomas had been the former chairman of the U.S. Equal Employment Opportunity Commission, the government agency charged with the responsibility for enforcing the federal laws prohibiting sexual harassment. During the confirmation hearing, Anita Hill, an ex-employee of the EEOC, made allegations that Thomas had sexually harassed her during the time he served as chairman of the EEOC.

Many have viewed the Thomas hearing as a watershed event—a public airing of the problem that created a new sensitivity to workplace harassment. It also prompted record numbers of women to come forward with their own complaints. Since the confirmation hearing, the number of workplace harassment charges filed against employers has increased fivefold.

What Is Illegal Sexual Harassment?

Title VII of the Civil Rights Act of 1964 makes sexual harassment illegal. It is considered to be a form of sex discrimination. The EEOC, headquartered in Washington, D.C., with district offices in most states and major cities in the United States, administers and enforces all federal employment discrimination laws and has issued detailed policy guidelines on issues of workplace harassment.

The EEOC's policy guidelines and court decisions generally regard sexual harassment to be any unwelcome verbal statements or physical conduct of a sexual nature that unreasonably interferes with another employee's job or work environment. The two most common types of illegal conduct are called *quid pro quo sexual harassment* and *hostile environment sexual harassment.* A third type of illegal conduct is called *third-party sexual harassment.*

The Three Types of
Illegal Sexual Harassment

- Quid pro quo sexual harassment
- Hostile environment sexual harassment
- Third-party sexual harassment

The lines between these types of harassment are not always clear, and the types of conduct often occur simultaneously. Precise legal guideposts—such as one sexually oriented joke is legal, while two offensive remarks targeting a female subordinate is not—do not exist in this context. What is clear is that the law is continuously evolving, notions of appropriate workplace behavior are changing, and a record number of claims—over 15,000—are being brought against employers and managers each year.

Quid Pro Quo Sexual Harassment

This kind of harassment occurs when employment decisions on hiring, promotion, discipline, or termination are made on the basis of submission to or rejection of unwelcome sexual conduct. For example, if a supervisor requests sexual favors from an employee, she refuses, and the supervisor then terminates her on account of the refusal, the courts will conclude that the employee is a victim of quid pro quo sexual harassment. The important inquiry in this context is what is known as *job detriment*. Did the victim suffer some sort of actual economic injury as a result of the harassment?

Hostile Environment Sexual Harassment

This type of illegal sexual harassment occurs when conduct of a sexual nature creates an intimidating, hostile, or offensive working environment for an employee. It can take many forms, including abusing someone verbally; discussing sexual activities; commenting on an employee's physical attributes or appearance; uttering demeaning sexual terms; using crude, vulgar, or offensive language; making unseemly sexual gestures or motions; engaging in unnecessary touching; or doing any of these types of activities in combination or repeatedly over time. Unlike quid pro quo sexual harassment, an employee need not suffer a monetary loss in order to state a viable claim of hostile environment sexual harassment. Likewise, an employee can make the claim without having to show psychological injury—all that is necessary is an adverse effect on one's work environment.

Courts focus on multiple factors in determining whether an employee's work environment is hostile in a legal sense. These factors include:

- How frequently the conduct was repeated
- Whether the conduct was blatantly offensive or severe
- Whether the conduct was physically threatening or humiliating
- Whether the conduct unreasonably interfered with an employee's work performance

In theory, a single isolated utterance of a sexual remark is usually insufficient to a prove a violation of Title VII. The law is not violated until there are multiple instances of similar conduct by an executive or supervisor toward one or more employees; over time, these incidents eventually will have a cumulative effect that poisons the work environment and therefore constitutes illegal harassment. In legal parlance, the conduct must be "severe" and "pervasive."

At the same time, a single event, such as an assault or threat of harm, may be so severe or intense as to violate the law without proof of any other inappropriate behavior. There is no rule per se or mathematical formula based on the number of offensive words or instances of misconduct. For this reason, it is critically important for managers to recognize that these factors do not create a clear test of or a precise guide for the multiplicity of situations that may arise in the workplace. Behavior that falls within any of these areas can lead to charges of sexual harassment. The line differentiating legal and illegal conduct is not black and white; it is distinctly fuzzy and consists of a spectrum of gray shaded areas

Third-Party Sexual Harassment

An emerging type of exposure for harassment concerns an employer's liability for the harassment of its employees by third parties such as customers, suppliers, and vendors. This is known as third-party sexual harassment. It is laden with liability.

The EEOC interprets Title VII to mean employers are

legally responsible for the acts of nonemployees in circumstances where the employer knew or should have known of the offending conduct. By continuing to expose its employees to a situation where sexual harassment has occurred in the past and is likely to occur in the future, the employer is deemed to be legally responsible for the third party's acts.

For this reason, managers need to be mindful of the conditions that employees are exposed to in this context. If an executive or supervisor has knowledge of the offending conduct, it is no defense to argue that "I was powerless to do anything because the harasser was not an employee of our company." A company must take affirmative steps in such circumstances to prevent any reoccurrence of the problem (e.g., by contacting the harasser's employer, banning the harasser from returning to the worksite, or safeguarding the affected employee).

The Difficulties in Defending Sexual Harassment Charges

The Invalid Defenses to Sexual Harassment

- Lack of intent to harass
- Conduct that is nonsexual in nature
- The harasser's right to express his or her views
- Absence of a formal complaint about harassment
- Conduct outside the workplace
- General conduct not focused on an intended victim
- The indiscriminate manager who treats men and women the same
- The relevance of a victim's off-duty conduct
- Consensual affairs

Employers have experienced considerable frustration and difficulty in responding to allegations of sexual harassment. In this respect, sexual harassment is easy to allege and often difficult to disprove. To avoid particular types of behaviors and situations that often lead to allegations of sexual harassment, managers need to appreciate that U.S. courts have consistently rejected various types of defenses in sexual harassment lawsuits. Managers should be mindful of the types of excuses and justifications the courts have rejected. These "workplace rules of the road" are shown below.

Lack of Intent to Harass

Courts have uniformly rejected the argument that there should be no liability for sexual harassment if the alleged harasser had no bad intent or meant no harm. Courts view conduct from the perspective of a reasonable person in the victim's shoes. The fact that the conduct at issue was done "in jest" or "as a joke" is irrelevant from a legal standpoint. If the effect of the conduct is to create an intimidating or hostile working environment, the fact that the harasser was simply joking or meant no harm will not excuse inappropriate behavior.

Conduct That Is Nonsexual in Nature

Courts also have rejected the defense that there should be no liability if the alleged harassing conduct is not sexual in nature. This is because the law is violated even if the harassment is not the product of sexual desire; instead, the critical factor is that the harassment takes place on account of an employee's sex. Therefore, there is no requirement that there be any physical touching or sexual overtures. If the employee was a target of the harassment because of his or her sex, this in and of itself constitutes illegal sexual harassment.

The Harasser's Right to Express His or Her Views

Some employers have attempted in the past to defend sexual harassment cases involving verbal statements on the notion that people have the right to "free speech" in the workplace and therefore such conduct cannot be illegal. Uninformed supervisors sometimes assume this too. This so-called defense is no defense at all and is a recipe for a legal disaster. Just as no one has the right to yell *fire* in a crowded theater and escape the legal consequences of injuries suffered by movie patrons fleeing in the ensuing panic, the right to free speech stemming from the U.S. Constitution can never justify verbal conduct in the workplace that results in sexual harassment.

Absence of a Formal Complaint about Harassment

Management personnel often assume that if no one complains about harassing conduct, then sexual harassment has not occurred. This is an incorrect assumption. A supervisor is absolutely liable for any act of sexual harassment that results in a subordinate suffering a tangible job detriment (e.g., a demotion, denial of a pay raise, etc.). Legal liability exists for an employer whenever a supervisor harasses a subordinate who suffers tangible job detriment or where the employer has actual or constructive knowledge of any other conduct constituting sexual harassment. A victim of such conduct need not complain to a manager. Persons who suffer in silence have valid claims too. Put simply, there is no legal defense to a sexual harassment charge based on the notion that "no one must have been offended" since "no one complained about it."

Conduct Outside the Workplace

Executives often believe that conduct occurring outside the workplace is a purely private matter. This is not the case with respect to certain forms of sexual harassment. It is no defense that such conduct is acceptable because it occurred off duty or off premises. This is on account of the 7/24/365 rule. For example, if a supervisor physically molests a female employee over a few drinks in a restaurant bar after work hours or on a business trip, illegal sexual harassment has occurred. As a supervisor, the harasser has apparent authority over the subordinate's terms and conditions of employment at all times.

General Conduct Not Focused on an Intended Victim

Courts have also rejected the defense that there should be no liability if the conduct is not directed at a particular female employee. Courts have held that so long as the harassing conduct occurs within the general vicinity of an employee, a viable sexual harassment claim may be asserted. For example, if several male employees recount their sexual behavior from a recent Friday night during a chance meeting in an office hallway, and a female employee is in the vicinity and overhears the statements and is offended by the discussion, this conduct may serve as the basis of a claim of hostile environment sexual harassment. This is despite the fact that the female employee did not participate in the discussion and the male employees did not intend that their conduct be aimed at or directed to the female employee.

The Indiscriminate Manager Who Treats Men and Women the Same

Employers sometimes attempt to defend a supervisor's harassing conduct on the grounds that the supervisor "treats everyone the same"—that, in essence, the manager indiscriminately treats male and female employees in an offensive manner. This is sometimes known as the *Archie Bunker defense*. Courts have rejected the notion that an indiscriminate manager may treat employees in this fashion without violating Title VII. The fact that a male supervisor uses sexual epithets in dealing with male employees does not justify such conduct when it is directed toward female workers. Such conduct can constitute sexual harassment.

The Relevance of a Victim's Off-Duty Conduct

Employers have often attempted to defend sexual harassment cases on the ground that alleged conduct of a sexual nature could not have been offensive to a particular female employee since she acts in a provocative nature off the worksite with respect to her own clothing, speech, or behavior. This defense is no defense at all. Courts generally have rejected the suggestion that a female employee's off-duty conduct—even if it is promiscuous—is relevant to whether or not an employer is liable for harassment directed toward her in the workplace. This is because no matter how promiscuous a female employee may be while off duty, this does not signal lawful acquiescence to unwanted sexual overtures and advances in the workplace. In essence, a female employee can never be deemed to "invite" sexual conduct by male coworkers based on her off-duty behavior.

Consensual Affairs

A private, consensual sexual relationship between a supervisor and a subordinate does not constitute sexual harassment. The element of "unwelcome" conduct is absent in this situation. However, office affairs exist in the legal danger zone of sexual harassment law. This is apparent on several levels. First, office affairs often lead to charges of favoritism. Coworkers may perceive that a supervisor treats the subordinate with whom he or she is having a romantic relationship in a biased fashion. In turn, this can lead to resentment and diminished morale and productivity. Second, problems stemming from a failed office affair or the souring of such a relationship create prime conditions for sexual harassment liability. Generally, courts have rejected the notion that an employee cannot complain of sexual harassment because of a prior consensual affair. Once a relationship turns sour, courts have often sided with employees who thereafter claim that they are the victims of sexual harassment when supervisors have treated them adversely in making personnel decisions after the relationship ends. Employees have the right to sever such relationships at any time without suffering retaliation or harassment on the job. Third, adverse treatment of the subordinate employee by other supervisors or coworkers can also prompt sexual harassment liability. This is because courts have determined that a female employee involved in an office affair can complain of sexual harassment if she is treated adversely by others. This is based on the notion that an employee's private and consensual sexual activities do not waive the legal protections against sexual harassment perpetrated by other supervisors and coworkers.

This summary of invalid defenses to charges of sexual harassment is instructive. It underscores the breadth of the legal prohibitions of federal, state, and local laws. It also illustrates the variety of excuses that managerial personnel are apt to hear from their subordinates in justifying their misconduct. As should be readily apparent, verbal statements or physical conduct are never justified if their effect is to create an abusive or hostile work environment.

Legitimate Defenses to Various Sexual Harassment Charges

The available defenses to sexual harassment charges are quite limited. However, none of the defenses is as effective as this simple guide to employee relations—always treat one's subordinates with respect, dignity, and empathy.

In quid pro quo sexual harassment cases, an employer's options in defending the case include demonstrating that no sexual advances occurred; if such advances did occur, the behavior was not unwelcome; if unwelcome sexual advances occurred, the plaintiff suffered no job detriment; or any job detriment the plaintiff suffered was not on account of the rejection of the sexual advances. The defense of this type of case is highly fact-sensitive and usually focuses on the element of unwelcomeness. Generally there is no direct evidence in cases where the sexual conduct took place in a one-on-one situation involving only the alleged harasser and the victim. The defense of these cases therefore becomes a "he-said–she-said" battle of sworn statements. The jury is usually left to judge the credibility of the witnesses in order to determine what actually happened behind closed doors.

In hostile work environment sexual harassment cases, employers usually defend such charges by disputing one or more elements of the plaintiff's case—whether or not the incidents of alleged sexual harassment took place; whether or not the incidents were sufficiently offensive, severe, or pervasive so as to alter the conditions of the worker's employment; or whether or not the employer has legal responsibility for the alleged conduct on account of a prompt investigation, the institution of immediate remedial measures, or the victim's failure to access readily available complaint procedures in a timely fashion.

In third-party sexual harassment cases, employers may

challenge the requirement of notice (that the employer knew or should have known of the problem) or defend their conduct on the grounds that they acted reasonably in trying to prevent any future instances of harassment.

As should be apparent, an executive or supervisor is often placed in a very difficult defensive posture in a sexual harassment case. The case often boils down to a simple swearing match consisting of the alleged victim testifying that the harassing conduct occurred and was unwelcome or pervasive, and the alleged harasser denying or minimizing the incident, or testifying that the interaction was consensual, invited, or not unwelcome. The typical scenario is the she-says–he-says situation. The alleged harasser is put in the untenable position of proving a negative—"I didn't do it" or "It's not as it seems."

Liability Stemming from Sexual Harassment

A sexual harassment claim can result in significant monetary loss to employers and managers. Such a claim is relatively easy for an employee to allege. It is costly to defend and often difficult to disprove.

Title VII allows any victim of sexual harassment to sue for compensatory and punitive damages. Sexual harassment victims need not suffer a "pocketbook" injury in order to bring a lawsuit. Mere exposure to conduct that constitutes sexual harassment entitles a plaintiff to sue for recovery of damages for the emotional distress and suffering attributable to being a victim of harassment. Such monetary awards can be quite substantial. Newspaper reports are replete every year with verdicts and settlements in excess of $1 million; the record to date is an $81 million verdict, although it was reduced by an appellate court to $3.5 million.

Victims of sexual harassment also can recover damages for lost salary in an amount equal to the compensation they would have earned had they not been subjected to illegal sexual harassment. This is known as *back-pay damages*. In a discharge case, back-pay damages are generally equivalent to the amount of money the victim has lost since being fired (and minus the compensation the victim has earned with a subsequent employer or should have earned had the ex-employee exercised reasonable diligence to mitigate the damages).

Many sexual harassment cases involve a *constructive discharge* situation. This occurs where a victim quits her or his job rather than face continual exposure to sexual harassment. The courts will treat the resignation as tantamount to a discharge if the harassment was sufficiently severe that any reasonable person in the worker's position would have felt compelled to quit. In these circumstances, potential back-pay damages are the same as if the plaintiff had been fired by the employer.

Courts also have the power under Title VII to impose equitable relief against employers. If an employee suffered a demotion or constructive discharge, the court has the authority to order the employer to promote the plaintiff or to provide reinstatement to the previous job. Many times, this relief also takes the form of a mandatory order to eliminate sexual harassment from the workplace. In essence, the court becomes involved in the internal operations of the company in order to monitor efforts to stop harassment in the workplace.

Finally, victims of alleged sexual harassment often use criminal assault and battery charges as a strategy to assist in their civil lawsuits for sexual harassment. In these circumstances, the employee will swear out a criminal assault and battery charge against an executive or supervisor. Oftentimes, the employee also will seek a court order of protection requiring the employer to keep the alleged harasser away from the employee. The executive or supervisor then faces potential criminal liability as well as a civil lawsuit.

Legal Strategies to Avoid Charges of Sexual Harassment

Court decisions and the EEOC's policy guidelines indicate that the best possible corporate defense to a charge of sexual harassment is for an employer to have an anti–sexual harassment personnel policy and complaint procedure. Without such a personnel policy, it is very difficult for an employer to defend against sexual harassment charges. Prudent executives and supervisors must ensure that the policy is enforced and followed by each and every employee. In a sense, it is the job responsibility of managers to ensure that all employees are treated with respect, empathy, and dignity, and in a manner consistent with the company's personnel policy.

The policy should define sexual harassment, prohibit such conduct as a matter of company policy, provide multiple avenues for aggrieved employees to make immediate complaints regarding what they believe to be sexual harassment, assure and protect the confidentiality of the complainant to the extent possible, prevent retaliation against any complaining party, and authorize prompt disciplinary action against any harassers. Information about the policy and the multiple avenues and methods for bringing an internal complaint must be thoroughly disseminated to all employees. To avoid liability under Title VII, an employer and its managers must immediately investigate any complaints of sexual harassment, and where warranted, institute prompt remedial measures designed to prevent any future reoccurrence of sexual harassment. Those remedial measures are wide and varied, and can range from outright termination of the harasser to bonus or salary reductions or mandatory counseling sessions.

Training and education for employees is equally important in reducing sexual harassment problems. Employers that invest in best-workplace-practices training programs receive "credit in the courthouse" for their efforts. Employees must be made aware that federal, state, and local employment discrimination laws prohibit harassment on the basis of sex as well as due to membership in any other protected categories (i.e., race, religion, age, etc.).

Preventing Sexual Harassment

In the courtroom, an attorney questions an executive accused of sexual harassment:

> *A: As you are well aware, my client has alleged that you propositioned her in your office while brushing up against her breasts with your hands.*
>
> *E: That's what she has claimed, but it is a lie; I didn't do that.*
>
> *A: You are also aware, are you not, that my client claims that after she rejected your overtures, you denied her a promotion and pay raise?*
>
> *E: I've read the allegations, and while I denied your client a promotion and pay raise, it wasn't because of anything she now alleges. It was due to her poor job performance.*
>
> *A: As an executive at your company, you know that sexual harassment is wrong and illegal, right?*
>
> *E: Absolutely. It's prohibited by law, and against company policy.*
>
> *A: And the company's policy applies to you, doesn't it?*
>
> *E: Certainly. It applies to everyone.*
>
> *A: Isn't it true that the policy states that the company will not tolerate any demeaning or offensive behavior that results in an abusive or hostile work environment?*
>
> *E: I don't know if that's an exact quotation, but our policy basically provides for that.*
>
> *A: You would agree that such a policy is important, wouldn't you?*
>
> *E: Yes, of course.*

A: *And isn't it true that as a supervisor, one of your respon-*
sibilities is to make sure company policy is enforced and
abided by?

E: *Well, sort of, but I think it's the HR Department's job to*
enforce a personnel policy.

A: *You're not serious are you? If you saw a male employee sex-*
ually assault a female employee, are you telling this jury
that you'd ignore it and justify your failure to do some-
thing by rationalizing that the HR Department has the
responsibility to put a stop to it?

E: *Well, I guess I would try to stop something like that.*

A: *And the reason you'd do so is because sexual harassment is*
both illegal and against company policy, and as a repre-
sentative of management, you want to make sure that em-
ployees abide by company policy and the law?

E: *Yes, I guess I agree.*

A: *Well, now that we've clarified your critical responsibilities*
as a management representative of the company, let's talk
about how you've fulfilled your responsibilities. In partic-
ular, let's talk about your e-mail communications.

E: *I don't see what that has to do with anything.*

A: *Well, let's let the jury decide that. I'm now going to show*
you plaintiff's group exhibit A, which consists of copies of
printouts of eight e-mails; you authored these e-mails,
didn't you?

E: *No, not really.*

A: *Isn't it a fact that these e-mails originated from the com-*
puter on your desk?

E: *Yes, but I received those messages from others.*

A: *And you then forwarded them to others, didn't you?*

E: *Well, yes, I forwarded these messages to three of my friends*
in the Finance Department.

A: *These were all jokes of a sexual nature, weren't they?*

E: *Well, sort of.*

A: *Please read to the jury your forwarding note from the last*
e-mail message.

E: *It says "You'll like this one. It reminds me of the blond in*
the typing pool with the huge t__s."

A: The two missing letters from the last word of your message are "i" and "t," correct?

E: Yes.

A: Now you're married and have two children, one of whom is a teenage girl, don't you?

E: Yes; but again, how is that relevant?

A: If an employee typed an e-mail that said this joke reminded him of your daughter's "t_ _s," do you think you, your wife, or daughter would find that to be demeaning or offensive?

E: Well, maybe.

A: Wouldn't you deem that this employee had acted inconsistently with the notion that your daughter is entitled to dignity and respect as a person?

E: I don't understand what you mean.

A: Would you agree that people, including those who work for you, are entitled to be treated with respect and dignity?

E: Again, I don't understand what you are questioning me about—what does this have to do with anything?

A: Well, then let's talk about something I hope you can understand. Let's talk about your company's Christmas party.

E: Sure. But what's that got to do with anything?

A: Last year a band provided entertainment after the dinner, right?

E: Yes.

A: You danced with several female colleagues, didn't you?

E: Yes; everybody was dancing.

A: In one of the dances, you told your dance partner she looked great, and that you'd like a Christmas kiss under the mistletoe, right?

E: Yes, but it was a joke. I didn't mean it.

A: You didn't mean it when you told her she looked pretty or when you said you'd like a kiss?

E: Well, the kiss part. I think I had too much to drink that night.

A: So if you were under the influence of alcohol, that would excuse it?

E: I didn't say that; I said I was just kidding.

A: *Isn't it true that if you drove an automobile while you were drunk, that would violate the law?*

E: *Well . . .*

A: *If you injured someone through your violation of the law, the fact that you were drunk or didn't mean to violate the law would be quite irrelevant, wouldn't it?*

E: *I'm not a lawyer, so I don't know.*

A: *Well, you have a driver's license, don't you, and you endeavor to follow the rules of the road, don't you?*

E: *Yes, I suppose that's right.*

A: *So do you think having had too much to drink is a legitimate excuse for violating the laws against sexual harassment?*

E: *Well . . .*

A: *You know better, don't you?*

E: *[no audible response]*

The plaintiff's attorney in this case then questioned the executive about all the other occasions he behaved in a manner inconsistent with the company's personnel policy. The plaintiff testified to the alleged encounter, which happened behind closed doors, while the executive denied it. In the closing argument, the plaintiff's attorney then posed the following rhetorical question to the jury:

A: *Given the evidence that came right out of the executive's mouth about those numerous instances where he uttered offensive remarks and treated employees with a lack of respect, do you believe him when he says "I didn't do it"?*

The Challenge

The line between illegal harassment and lawful yet immature or crude behavior is difficult to discern under the evolving law of sexual harassment. As a practical matter, this enables the plaintiff's lawyer to bring credible sexual harassment lawsuits involving less than credible circumstances. This is especially true in the he-said–she-said type of situation where all the conduct in question occurred behind closed doors and only two people really know what happened.

The dynamics of a he-said–she-said lawsuit illustrate the dangers of conduct that encroaches on the *fuzzy line* of sexual harassment. When the accused employee has to prove a negative (i.e., "I didn't do it"), the plaintiff's lawyer typically uses evidence of questionable behavior at other times, or in interactions with other employees, to cast doubt on the accused person's declaration of innocence.

If the jury perceives that this laundry list of insensitive remarks or offensive conduct is inconsistent with the expected code of office behavior, the jury is apt to side with the plaintiff. Usually this is because the jury gives the plaintiff the benefit of the doubt, based on the notion that the harasser's behavior on other occasions is circumstantial evidence that the harasser probably did it, as the plaintiff has claimed.

It should be apparent that any activity that comes anywhere near the fuzzy line between legal and illegal conduct should be strictly avoided by all managers and employees. But staying clear of the danger zone of hostile work environment sexual harassment is easier said than done.

In the vignette that began this chapter, we learned that the employer had an antiharassment policy, but it did not stop the problem from occurring or prevent it from getting worse over time. We do not know the end of this story. But this much we do know from the brief court record:

- The executive was aware of his employer's antiharassment policy.
- The plaintiff also knew the company policy, including what to do about sexual harassment.
- Coworkers in the office had knowledge of the sexual harassment—at least once at the holiday party and over the course of eight e-mails to multiple employees in the Finance Department.

Any one of these people, at any time, *could* have done something to alter the course of events in this case, but no one did. This is not unusual in cases of hostile work environment sexual harassment. It is often a "family secret" that coworkers, including managers, are aware of but keep to themselves.

Sexual harassment is the number-one claim brought before the EEOC *every* year. Hostile work environment harassment, unlike procedural forms of discrimination, is based on perception. It is much harder to change what employees *think* than it is to change what they *do*.

When the courts pull the engine of social change at a speed faster than people can keep up with, some companies just can't make the needed changes quickly enough. Laws change faster than people do. The courts demand a "new order" in the workplace. But it remains for the rest of us to figure out how to adapt ourselves to be in compliance with the law.

The tail wags the dog.

The way change happens, it is easier to modify the public voice, the socially correct way to think and feel, than it is the private voice, the way people *really* think and feel. Consequently, in the United States the first major training efforts have been devoted to changing the public voice of American workers.

We have been very successful in building a national rhetoric that prohibits gender discrimination. The proof is that virtually no group of workers evokes more "political correctness" today than women. Care in using gender-free language, avoiding sexist jokes, and making other accommodations is a barometer to women workers that gender equity is on the front burner of the public mind.

But statistics on hostile work environment sexual harassment tell us how much farther we have to go to change the private voice. This chapter is written to help managers make sense out of an area of business practice that defies common sense. Conflicts of interest, the absence of a "right" answer, ambiguity of intentions and definitions, and lack of preparation make it difficult for the proactive supervisor to know *how* to be helpful in preventing hostile work environment sexual harassment.

Manager's Definition of Hostile Work Environment Sexual Harassment

Starting with the rule of thumb we apply to all forms of hostile work environment harassment including gender, the harassment *complaint* should not be confused with the harassment *problem*. When hostile work environment sexual harassment occurs, it is symptomatic of a more pervasive problem with employee respect in the company.

Preventing sexual harassment is therefore a matter of discovering where the true problem lies. The important question for the manager is, *who* in the organization is responsible for *what* part of the hostile environment sexual harassment?

In most corporations, human resources (or another assigned agent) records, investigates, and corrects sexual harassment *complaints*. HR oversees the employer's public voice—its anti-harassment policy and complaint procedure.

The private voice is more difficult to monitor. It is what employees really think and feel, sometimes below their level of awareness, but what they express indirectly in their work relationships. The employer has no direct contact with the private voice. It falls to managers to oversee its harmony with the public voice in the day-to-day interactions among the employees they supervise.

The manager's definition of hostile work environment sexual harassment is therefore different from that of human resources. HR has a *procedural* definition, based on compliance to the corporation's policy. The manager has an *interpersonal* definition. It is based on how employees treat one another. When the two are not in alignment, the risk of an employee incident increases.

Using the manager's definition, two conditions must be met for hostile work environment sexual harassment to occur:

1. The two employees in the harassment dispute must have a conflict between their public and private voices.

    This means they are saying one thing but doing another. From our research, we learned that both parties in the hostile environment exchange usually know the rules on how to treat people based on

gender. This is their public voice. But privately, they may not agree
with the rules, or may not believe their behavior violates them.

We call the first condition *misalignment of the public and private voice*.

2. The two employees must be unaware of how their misalignment is
expressed in their behavior toward one another.

This means they are in the dark about how they come off to the
other person. From our research, we also learned that employees
who get enmeshed in hostile work environment sexual harassment
episodes usually do not see how their private voices drive their behavior. Because this is true for both employees, they are "double
blind."

We call them a *harassment couple* because the sexual harassment grows out of their *interaction*, not the misperceptions of
either party alone.

We reserve the term *harassment couple* for protagonists in
cases of hostile work environment sexual harassment. We do
not apply it to the parties in cases of supervisor harassment,
or in the extreme, workplace sexual assault. In these cases,
there is a clear "victim" who has less power than the "aggressor." Neither of these conditions is necessarily met in
cases of hostile work environment harassment. Instead, we
most often encounter a complicated patchwork of communications, misunderstandings, and allegations where "no one is
all right" and "everyone feels wronged."

In the double-blind hostile work environment sexual harassment couple, the misalignment between public and private voices spells risk. The key to prevention is to help managers spot and correct misalignments between employees in
their departments before an interpersonal problem escalates
into a formal sexual harassment complaint.

Manager's Tool Kit

We will give the manager a tool kit to learn how to identify
critical misalignments between the public and private voices
that leave the company vulnerable to hostile work environ-

ment sexual harassment. These tools prevent such problems from erupting, or keep an existing problem from growing bigger. If a manager learns about an incident of hostile work environment sexual harassment, we recommend these seven steps to realign the perceptions of the accuser and the accused in relation to the organization.

Step 1. Align the Public and Private Voices of the Accuser

Follow These Steps to Accomplish Step 1

To bring greater alignment of the public and private voices of the accuser, we recommend that the manager:

- Reassure the accuser that sexual harassment is not tolerated in the company.
- Reassure the accuser that sexual harassment behavior is one of the inappropriate ways some workers express personal hostility and frustration. Make sure that the employee knows you value his or her contribution. Though you are not a counselor, try to find out if the employee perceives problems that go beyond the harassment complaint.
- Reassure the accuser that he or she is not alone.

When the manager provides this support, accusers can still be mistrustful (the manager could be the harasser's friend) or angry (why didn't the manager protect me in the first place?). Supervisors must understand these reactions and assure the employee *I am going to try to make this place safe for you.*

In the first stage of hostile work environment sexual harassment, the misalignment is between the public and private voices of the employee accuser. Let us start with the public voice. Sexual harassment victims are far less isolated in the workplace than they once were. National attention has been showered on gender sensitivity over the past decade, and most American workers have had at least a few crash courses in what to do if they are being sexually harassed.

The public voice in America "knows" what sexual harassment is!

Based on years of counseling employers and consulting to corporations across the country, however, we are struck by the fact that despite heightened awareness of sexual harassment and well-publicized incidence rates of anywhere between 35 to over 50 percent of all working women, victims are inevitably *surprised* when it happens to them.

Their private voice is clearly not in alignment with the media!

Many victims of sexual harassment report being even more surprised by how they *feel*. Countless women (and a few men) have confided in us that they did not expect to react to the harassment as strongly as they did. Although they were aware of the issues, they were not prepared for it to happen to them.

These victims have a disconnect between a strong public voice that is closely attuned to the detection and identification of sexual harassment and a private voice that says, "It won't happen to me." When we try to explain this misalignment in sexual harassment victims, we come up with a few hypotheses.

Maybe the private voice is really skeptical and only pays lip service to the belief that sexual harassment is as big a problem as the politically correct public voice concedes. This person is genuinely surprised when sexual harassment happens to him or her.

Or maybe the private voice is the problem. Some victims strongly believe sexual harassment is wrong, but, for reasons of personal history, are prone to blame themselves anyway when it happens to them, no matter what the public voice advises. Here, the victim outwardly denounces the harassment but inwardly feels it is deserved.

Or is there another explanation why, for so many *ordinary* workers, the private voice defies the logic of the public voice, is surprised when harassment happens, and is even *more* surprised to discover how they feel about it?

We have a hint in the vignette that began the chapter. The he-said–she-said dispute is a very interesting phenomenon if we stop for a moment to reflect on it. When we reread the transcript it becomes apparent that the accused harasser experiences as much conflict as the accuser victim.

Hostile work environment harassment is always embedded in the broader context of a work relationship between the two employees. It is not a separate event, or a unique contract that can be cut from the stream of ongoing activities that the two people share at work. Thus the harassment victim usually has any number of contacts with the harasser, maybe even some positive, that have to be considered in the summary judgment of the whole relationship.

Misalignment between the public and private voices begins when the hostile work environment sexual harassment victim tries to apply legal standards to determine if the suspect behavior *is* or *is not* harassment. Relationships and interactions are complex and nuanced and cannot always be reduced to an easy "right" or "wrong" response.

The private voice of the victim is not so sure what sexual harassment *is*.

This does not mean that sexual harassment victims are necessarily unclear about the particular sexual harassment acts or their significance. The victim may be very sure that certain actions or events are intended as hostile and meet all the legal criteria for sexual harassment. But in most cases, these interactions are only part of a much more complicated picture, not all of which is negative or hostile.

Victims are just as likely to be responsible people as any other employees, and will automatically take ownership in their personal relationships—even those with harassers. It follows then that victims in cases of hostile work environment sexual harassment will hold themselves responsible for some part of the harassment problem, even if the courts do not. This is why most victims experience feelings of guilt.

The proactive manager can be helpful to the victim. It is not the manager's job to decide who is right or wrong in a sexual harassment incident. Human resources formally investigates the sexual harassment complaint. It is the manager's job to explore the perceptions of the victim that lead up to the sexual harassment problem. Are there still disagreements among employees in the department after the sexual harassment incident is resolved?

Specifically, if you are supervising a sexual harassment victim, inquire if this employee feels generally respected by his or her coworkers. Have there been any changes in the department that have upset the balance in the work group? Are there conflicts that you are unaware of that may be fueling a harassment problem?

On a final note, it is usual for victims to feel confused about their sexual harassment experience and afraid of what other employees will think of them. Managers can provide a "safe" environment and encourage victims to talk about these reactions. If an employee persists in feeling guilty or isolating himself or herself for a long time, it may be beneficial to recommend that the employee seek professional advice from human resources.

Step 2. Align the Public and Private Voices of the Accused

Follow These Steps to Accomplish Step 2

To bring greater alignment of the public and private voices of the accused, we recommend that the manager meet with the employee and:

- Explain that sexual harassment is not tolerated in the company. Avoid talking about the actual incident or naming names. Investigating the harassment complaint is the job of human resources. Your goal is to reassure the harasser that you are there to protect all employees in the department.
- Explain that sexual harassment behavior is one of the inappropriate ways some workers express personal hostility and frustration. Explore with the harasser what his or her frustrations are. Try to see if the worker can shift perception and see interactions from the other person's perspective. The harassment complaint is probably not the only employee problem.
- Explain how *no one* is respected in the department unless *everyone* is accepted. The harasser needs to be part of the team.

When the manager provides this support, the harasser is indirectly put on notice about the harassment conduct, and the issues that underlie it are also put on the table. This reduces the harasser's isolation and lessens the chances of continued harassment. If you find it difficult to follow this step, pay close attention to steps 3 and 4 and learn why.

In cases of hostile work environment sexual harassment, the public and private voices of the harasser are also in misalignment. Most harassers we have known do not perceive their conduct as illegal harassment, and are surprised or even angered when accusations are made against them.

The public voice says, "It was just a joke!"

We use this statement metaphorically, of course, but not accidentally. It is no mistake that this rejoinder has become a part of the national lexicon of sexual harassment humor. When a statement becomes a common saying, it has a meaning that we all intuitively understand.

This is a good example of our private voice! We know more than we think we know about sexual harassers, and that knowledge is conveyed through humor and metaphor.

Here is the riddle. On average, it is a safe assumption that accused harassers have as much training and education in sexual harassment as their victims. Why is there a difference between *their* public voices, which say they are just kidding, and those of their *accusers*, who claim they are harassers?

Here is the answer we hear all the time. Unlike other employees:

Sexual harassers "just don't get it."

This is the average person's assessment of the harasser's private voice. The belief is so widespread, it deserves entry into the national register of sexual harassment idioms. Like the first entry, "just don't get it" also communicates a message about harassers that we intuitively understand. Our private voice is helping us out once more, and leading the way on our path of inquiry. Let's follow it.

We ask ourselves, what precisely is it that harassers just "don't get"?

We have known many sexual harassers. There is nothing especially dense about the ones we have worked with. Oftentimes, they are stellar employees who occupy important positions in their companies. They have spouses, families, and good incomes. What stops them from understanding what ordinary people "get," without any trouble, that sexual harassment is wrong?

Our public voice has let us down! We cannot find a logical answer to the riddle. We do not know what it is that the harasser doesn't get; and *we* don't get the harasser's humor when he or she defends misconduct with the retort, "It was just a joke!"

Maybe our private voice knows the answer. Rather than follow logic, let's follow our intuition. The solution to the riddle is right in front of our eyes. It is in the idioms. They reveal some very simple but profound truths about sexual harassers that we all know, but don't know that we know.

This is what gets sexual harassers into trouble.

- *"It was just a joke."* Psychological research teaches us that hostile work environment sexual harassers are unaware of their own private voices. They deny having any hostile feelings toward their victims, at least at the time the harassment occurred.

This is why they do not *feel* their behavior is hostile. When we cannot hear our private thoughts, we do not know how we come off to others. We then do not apply appropriate brakes to inappropriate self-expression.

- *"They just don't get it."* This belies another simple truth. There *is* something very important that harassers do not get. It is the message of the victim's private voice.

Harassers are generally poor at reading cues. They do not perceive the victim's signals accurately and therefore fail to back off when others would see the handwriting on the wall.

There are complex psychological reasons why some people cannot "hear" their private motivations or "read" cues from other people. But managers are not therapists. It is not their job to conduct investigations, like human resources does, or solve the harasser's personal problems, like counselors do. There is, however an important role they can play to help safeguard the department from continued harassment problems and to assist the harasser in recovering.

We suggest that supervisors accept a few givens about hostile work environment sexual harassers. Sexual harassers are most often defensive about their conduct because they are missing important pieces of information. This is what got them into trouble in the first place. Angry and ashamed at the accusation of sexual harassment, they cover up.

If you are supervising a sexual harasser, try to explore the harasser's perceptions of important interactions he or she is having with coworkers. If sexual harassment is a problem, you can bet this worker has more general problems with respect. Instead of assuming the employee is purposefully antagonistic to coworkers, reexplain to the harasser a suspect interaction. Can the harasser view the situation differently with your guidance?

If the harasser can shift perception, there is a good chance that he or she can be helped to improve workplace interactions. If not, listen to your private voice! Read the cues and back off. This is an employee who is at risk for continued harassment problems.

Step 3. Align the Public and Private Voices of the Manager about the Victim

Follow These Steps to Accomplish Step 3

To bring greater alignment of your public and private voices about the victim, we recommend that you:

- Explore your feelings about potential retaliation if you come forward and acknowledge the victim's experience. Do you believe you have your employer's full support? Are you secretly also afraid of the harasser?
- Explore your feelings about the harassment incident and ask yourself if you are able to be an impartial supervisor. Be aware that it is common to blame the victim when harassment occurs. This means we look for a "reason" why the harassment happened to the particular employee. We do this when the situation makes us feel very uncomfortable.
- Seek the help of a trusted friend or colleague to talk to about these issues to make sure that you are not blind to some bias that could keep you from helping and supporting the victim.

When managers take stock of their own feeling of security in the organization and of their personal reactions to the victims of sexual harassment, they are better able to help the employee. Getting a second opinion on your perception is good prevention. It protects you and the victim.

Managers sometimes have trouble completing steps 1 and 2. When this happens, it may be because like harassers and victims, supervisors also have a public and private voice when it comes to hostile work environment sexual harassment. Moreover, when their voices are misaligned, the supervisors are less able to respond empathically to either of the parties in the harassment couple.

Because of the important role managers play in preventing sexual harassment, it is worth their while to take a moment and do a self-check to discover if they have any roadblocks that stand in the way of effective supervision. Some of these are quite common. We underscore they are reactions that *ordinary* people have.

Let's start at the beginning. There is a complex set of psychological reactions managers experience that causes them to hold back from getting involved in sexual harassment problems with their employees. The mere accusation of *harassment* sounds an emotional alarm in the private voice, and managers feel vulnerable. How should they handle the situation? Will it impact on them?

In cases of hostile work environment sexual harassment, it is easy for the supervisor to turn a deaf ear to the problem. The he-said–she-said dispute lends itself very nicely to rationalization by the uncomfortable manager. The allegations are hard to substantiate by facts and are therefore easily dismissed as rumor or exaggeration.

Besides, can managers themselves boast that they *never* told an off-color joke or made a sexist remark?

The similarity the manager perceives between himself or herself and either the victim or the harasser is psychologically too close for comfort. In an attempt to gain some emotional distance from unwanted identifications with the helplessness of the victim *or* the aggression of the harasser, the manager minimizes the harassment situation as "misperception" or "overreaction." This is what most often leads to misalignment.

We call these biases in perception *normative distortions*. Why?

First, because they are *normal*. This means that most people experience them. Second, they are *distortions* because they are typical ways of bending perception so that our impression fits what we want to see. Normative distortions are below the threshold of awareness. Therefore managers do not know when they happen.

This can be a very serious problem. When managers interpret the interpersonal problems of the harassment couple through a veil of their own normative distortion, they are less able to be reliable "mirrors." Employees lose an opportunity to correct *their* distortions, and managers lose empathy for employees.

Now let's take a look at how this affects the manager's perception of the sexual harassment victim. Remember, the supervisor's task in step 1 is to explore with this employee how the employee perceives her or his relationships at work. If managers are biased in how they perceive *victims*, how can they be *objective* in helping employees see themselves in relation to others?

We begin to appreciate how a manager's biases can contaminate the supervision process. The most common normative distortion of managers who supervise accusers is "blaming the victim." When this occurs, we feel that the victim is in some way inviting the harassment, or is not doing enough to stop it. The misaligned manager consciously or unconsciously takes sides against the victim. This not only is prohibited by the employer but also is not conducive to a positive supervisory relationship.

Blaming the victim is a curious phenomenon. From our research on the perception of sexual harassment victims, we learned that the more helpless we perceive a victim to be, the more likely we are to blame him or her for being in that predicament. This means that employees lose empathy most dramatically for "weak" victims and do not want to be associated with them.

Of course, we do not like to admit to these feelings out loud. They contradict the rules of conscience of the public voice that say it is wrong to blame the helpless. But managers are people. And they will act on these feelings in subtle ways if they are experiencing them. Bias inevitably clouds vision. Supervisors who blame the victim may, for example, look the other way, minimize the employee's experience, or overprotect the accuser. These distortions get in the way of the victim's recovery.

If you are supervising a sexual harassment victim, it is important for you to explore your private voice. Do you blame the victim? We recommend that managers talk about their perceptions to a third party, either a trusted friend or a person assigned by the employer. It is also sometimes helpful to seek guidance from human resources on how to supervise harassment victims to be sure that you know the boundaries of confidentiality. Get some tips on how to be helpful.

Your job as manager in supervising a harassment victim is to provide support and reassurance that you value the employee. You should not take sides. Try to understand that when sexual harassment occurs, victims feel generally disrespected on the job. Find out what the employee needs to feel secure, and, if appropriate, try to make necessary corrections to improve the work atmosphere.

Step 4. Align the Public and Private Voices of the Manager about the Harasser

Follow These Steps to Accomplish Step 4

To bring greater alignment of your public and private voices about the harasser, we recommend that you:

- Explore your feelings about potential retaliation if you directly acknowledge the harassment. Are you afraid of the harasser's hostility? Will your employer be displeased if you upset the applecart by paying attention to a problem that the company wants to minimize?
- Explore your feelings about the harasser and ask yourself if you are able to be an impartial supervisor. Be aware that it is common for managers to fear becoming the harasser's next victim. This fear becomes even stronger if the employer minimizes the problem.
- Seek the help of a trusted friend or colleague to talk to about these issues to make sure that you are not blind to some bias that could get in the way of your helping the harasser and preventing future harassment episodes.

When managers take stock of their own sense of vulnerability, they are in a better position to supervise the sexual harasser with empathy and impartiality. Because this can be a very difficult task, we advise all managers to get a second opinion on their perceptions. It protects you and the accused.

Misalignment of the public and private voice is common in relation to sexual harassers. Supervising these employees may be one of the more difficult challenges undertaken by the manager. Therefore, it is worth taking a moment to think about how you define your goals as a supervisor after an accusation of hostile work environment sexual harassment has been lodged against a worker in your department.

Just as we saw with victims, there are also some rather common normative distortions in the manager's perception of sexual harassers. When these distortions occur, managers are less able to be effective in the supervisory process. One of the more common problems is "identification with the aggressor." When this occurs, we acknowledge that the harasser's behavior may be inappropriate, or even ridiculous, but it is not really "harassment." In an attempt to gain psychological distance from the feeling of threat that the harasser evokes unconsciously, the supervisor takes sides with the harasser. Most significantly from a prevention point of view, when this happens the supervisor inadvertently validates the harasser's behavior, making the problem still harder for the organization to correct.

Another common distortion is "writing off" the harasser. Here, the supervisor gives up on the employee, deciding the harasser is hopeless and can't change. This reaction works in a tricky way. The manager, like the victim, is reacting internally to the harasser's hostility. Whether or not the manager is aware of it, openly acknowledging the harassment as aggression is likely to invite the harasser's hostile defense—like waving a red flag in front of a charging bull. Not wanting to become the *next* target of the harasser's hostility, the supervisor denies or minimizes the impact of the harassment.

This has obvious negative consequences for all parties involved. The harasser is left to his or her own devices to figure out what is going wrong. This is useless, since difficulty reading cues is what got the harasser into trouble in the first place! And the increased isolation caused by the supervisor's "desertion" only intensifies the harasser's anger at being "punished." On full consideration, this supervisory dynamic actually *raises* the threshold of possible recurrence of harassment conduct.

It is easy to see the downside of these perceptual biases. They not only interfere with the manager's clarity of perception, but also influence the supervisory relationship in a direction away from prevention. The misaligned manager of a harasser surrenders a critical opportunity to help that employee confront his or her problem realistically, with the help of an objective person.

We begin to appreciate how important the supervisor is in preventing a harassment incident from becoming a harassment crisis. If you are supervising a sexual harasser, we recommend that you talk to a trusted friend or a third party assigned by the corporation to make sure that your private voice is not influencing you in ways that interfere with the forming of a helpful work relationship.

Talk to human resources to get some tips on how to evaluate the risk in your department. Do not attempt to manage this job alone—it takes advanced skill to supervise this employee effectively, and the outcome is too important!

Step 5. Align the Private Voices of the Victim and the Employer

---

Follow These Steps to Accomplish Step 5

To bring greater alignment of the private voices of the victim and the employer, we recommend that, as a manager, you:

- Make sure that you follow the company's antiharassment policy and report all known incidents of sexual harassment. Under no circumstances is it to anyone's advantage to ignore a victim, especially one whom you also supervise.
- Make sure you follow up with victims who are harassed in your department. While you are not responsible for correcting the sexual harassment incident, you are responsible to be on the watch for other manifestations of the harassment problem.
- Make sure you share your observations with your employer. Use the harassment incident to leverage improvements for the department. This helps the victim and ultimately the whole company.

When managers fulfill their function as intermediaries, they shift the focus from the victim to the organization. Make suggestions to the employer about how to improve the work atmosphere. Your department may benefit from the harassment experience.

We are rounding the bend of the manager's job in the re-alignment of public and private voices. It is time to look up the corporate ladder to executive leadership. As we noted earlier, supervisors are intermediaries in the organization. They translate the policies set forth by the employer to the workers they supervise, and they carry information from the workers back to executive leadership.

Just as managers are influenced by their public and private voices when supervising harassment couples, the company's public and private voices also play a role in preventing further harassment. The company's antiharassment policy and complaint procedure informs its public voice. Its private voice is measured in the resources the employer allocates to training and monitoring the effectiveness of its compliance program.

Most companies today have public and private voices that are in good alignment when it comes to sexual harassment. They have policies in place. They are engaged in training personnel. They have complaint procedures and EEO officers who tally and monitor the effectiveness of these procedures.

In short, many companies are doing *everything right*. And still the incidence of hostile environment sexual harassment continues to rise. We offer a final riddle, this one for the employer:

When is it *wrong* to do everything *right?*

To figure this out, let's look historically at what employers actually did when confronted with the unsettling reality that "doing everything right" did not bring down the rates of sexual harassment litigation. In utter frustration, most did *more* of the same. Unable to directly control employee behavior, but not wanting to take the financial hit for occasional *mis*-behavior, they tightened the controls they already had in place. These are the company's policies and procedures. More threats and stricter punishment!

Employers grew less and less forgiving of harassers: There would be zero tolerance!

This term has become another popular idiom in the national sexual harassment lexicon. Again, there is simple truth in the saying. Our private voice is giving us the needed clue to solve the riddle.

The idiom reflects a typical employer response to the law. The public voice of the courts states the universal ideal: to create a workplace that is free of hostility and intimidation. The employer translates this by holding employees hostage to an ideal, with the counterpromise of zero tolerance.

Ideals are not real numbers. We *strive* for the ideal but *live* in the real. Most large companies will fail to achieve zero tolerance in the real world. Moreover, current business trends suggest that it will be even harder in the times to come than in the past. First, the work force is less stable. Businesses rely more than ever on consultants and outsourcing. In this transient landscape, it is difficult for the employer to know, much less monitor, employee interactions. Second, globalization adds to the diversity of public and private voices that come into play in the multinational corporation.

How have employers met these challenges to bridge the gap between the real and the ideal in a changing business climate?

American corporations have traditionally applied a *punishment model* to the treatment of sexual harassment. This is an ideology that is also borrowed from the law. Like the courts, the corporation's complaint procedure seeks to protect victims and apprehend offenders. This is appropriate for serious abusive acts or for crimes of sexual assault that are committed in the workplace.

But hostile work environment sexual harassment, as we have repeatedly pointed out, is not *absolute*. In most cases, we never discover the whole truth, if there is one truth to discover. Hostile work environment sexual harassment is about a *relationship* between employees.

Yet we continue to use a punishment model for these lesser crimes of workplace hostility, chasing after "culprits" and providing restitution to "victims." Terms like *zero tolerance* reinforce the belief that there is a rogue harasser profile and this employee *should* be punished.

Though research would tell us otherwise, the public voice demands that we label one member of the harassment couple the *culprit* and the other the *victim*. This is not so easily done. The employer is often backed into a position where a harasser's entire employment record, which may be excellent in many respects, is held to the standard of zero tolerance for sexual harassment allegations that seem less important than the bottom line. Under this kind of pressure the employer's public voice and private voice split.

What is the impact of the company's misalignment on the sexual harassment victim? We have already remarked that "winning" is psychologically very complicated for victims, who rarely blame their harassers for *all* that happened. When the private voice of the employer also blames the victim, the situation is more serious.

This is a tough spot for the manager. He or she is now sandwiched between an employee who needs support and understanding and an employer that wants to minimize the impact of the whole problem. The resolution of the contradiction is right before our eyes—if we stay focused. We have said repeatedly that sexual harassment is never the *real* problem, but is a *symptom* of a problem. If the manager has been successful in the first four steps, he or she has learned what the trigger points are in the department that have instigated the harassment symptom.

By shifting attention from the victim's reaction to the sexual harassment to remedying the organizational conflict that spawned it, the manager not only gets out of the middle, but also has a valuable opportunity to make a positive contribution to the growth of the company. Here is how to do it. Think of the harassment incident as an *example* of something negative that happened to an employee in your department. Shift the spotlight away from the *particular* victim. Ask yourself, as a supervisor, what would you do *differently* in hindsight to have prevented the sexual harassment?

You may come up with a few good answers. Then share your insights with your boss. Use the harassment as an opportunity to explore the growth needs of your department so that it is safeguarded against further hostility in the future. This is proactive thinking.

Your shift in focus also goes a long way to help the victim

recover and resume normal functioning on the job. It demonstrates that rehabilitation is often a better route than punishment—for the victim, the harasser, and the company as a whole. And finally, it models for other employees that finding solutions, and not looking for blame, is effective leadership.

Step 6. Align the Private Voices of the Harasser and the Employer

---

Follow These Steps to Accomplish Step 6

To bring greater alignment of the private voices of the harasser and the employer, we recommend that, as a manager, you:

- Make sure you follow the company's antiharassment policy and report all known incidents of sexual harassment. Under no circumstances is it to anyone's advantage to ignore a harasser, especially one whom you also supervise.
- Make sure you follow up with harassers. While you are not responsible for correcting the sexual harassment incident, you are responsible for trying to correct the sources of the hostility between employees in your department and for preventing avoidable future harassment episodes.
- Make sure you share your observations with your employer. Make a plan for the readjustment of the harasser in your department. Monitor its effectiveness with your employer.

When managers fulfill their function as intermediaries and communicate clearly to harassers and to their employers, they are safeguarding the company from further problems. You want to be a part of the solution, not a part of the problem.

It is the harasser's turn, again. What can the manager do to bring this employee in alignment with the company's private voice? The punishment model does not work any better for harassers than it does for victims. As we look closer, especially in the aftermath of a complaint, we see that punishment is even less productive than we thought.

Let's back up and look at the issue from the employer's perspective. It is the company's first obligation to protect the workplace against sexual harassment. To achieve this, the employer must evaluate the potential of the accused harasser to return to acceptable workplace behavior and stop the harassment conduct.

Will punishment help any of this?

To find out, we need to attune ourselves to the harasser's private voice. This is what we know. Assuming the investigation finds that he or she is the identified "culprit," harassers secretly believe *they* are the true victims. Why? Because without needed insight to fill in the gaps of misperception, they still do not entirely know what they did wrong. Harassers often feel as abused by "the system" as victims feel abused by them. In this state of mind, punishment will probably do more harm than good.

Moreover, punishment does not touch the harasser's real problem. This is an employee who has pervasive difficulty relating respectfully to others in the workplace. But only *some* of these interpersonal problems also qualify as harassment. A confused harasser will internally resist the employer's attempt at behavioral "correction."

The private voice of the harasser is not operating under the punishment model.

Shifting to a proactive approach, the manager can instead test the waters with the harasser to discover if change is possible, as we have described in step 4. But now we add another level to the process. It is most important for the supervisor to stay in close contact with the employer and give accurate feedback on the harasser's progress. If the employer determines to allow the harasser to continue employment, a model of progressive opportunity is the better way to go.

With the employer's input, the supervisor needs to develop a recovery plan for the harasser. This will of course vary depending on the person and the situation. Necessary beginning steps include restructuring the work environment to assure the security of coworkers during a trial period and establishing a process to regularly monitor the harasser. Some employers offer recovering harassers counseling through an employee assistance program or private resources. Formal evaluation by a forensic psychologist can also be helpful to get a reliable measure of harassment risk.

In short, the employer's offer of a second chance to the harasser is meaningless unless it is backed by a concrete plan that the supervisor oversees. Not only is this fair to the accused employee, but it also reduces the risk that the employer will be confronted later on with a lawsuit for wrongful termination if the harasser strikes again.

While the employer, not the supervisor, makes the final decision about the continued employment of the harasser, the outcome can only be as good as the information that the company is given. Not all harassers can or will change, even with the best of rehabilitation opportunities presented to them by the supervisor and the company.

The supervisor needs to document efforts made to promote recovery of the harasser and give the employer regular and reliable feedback to assist in the decision-making process. Following these steps protects you personally, protects the rights of the accused harasser to fair but progressive discipline, and builds the credibility of the company.

Step 7. Provide Employee Training

The most powerful resource the manager has to monitor the workplace for ongoing hostile work environment sexual harassment is coworkers. The very term *hostile environment* implies something profound about this form of sexual harassment. By definition, it is not limited to the harasser and victim. Subtle and pervasive manifestations of hostility— lewd pictures, offensive e-mail, off-color jokes, sexual comments—infect the whole work atmosphere.

If a hostile work environment is a "family affair," who better to monitor it than coworkers, the members of the family themselves?

Sexual harassment training should be done routinely in any circumstance if the employer hopes to have an affirmative defense against potential sexual harassment claims. But if a problem has already surfaced, training takes on a greater urgency.

Not any kind of training will do, however. When hostile work environment sexual harassment occurs, we have seen throughout this chapter that conflicts between and among the public and private voices of managers, victims, harassers, and coworkers are enough to raise the roof in a concert hall. Traditional training in the dos and don'ts will not reach all sections of the choir.

Coworkers are the most effective but least utilized resource to prevent sexual harassment.

Training is effective when employees are helped to explore their private voices in relation to company policy and the law. We have the methodology to measure and quantify employee perceptions of sexual harassment and guide workers to discover where their particular misalignments are. Training focuses specifically on realigning these critical perceptions so that they do not get in the way of self-protection or stop the employee from safeguarding others in the workplace.

What stops some employers and supervisors from advocating for this?

Ironically, the final layer of misalignment between public and private voice is between the laws of the land and the laws of human nature. The U.S. Supreme Court is the embodiment of the public voice and encourages a punishment model to treat sexual harassment. Employers translate this into antiharassment policies and complaint procedures to settle disputes between antagonistic employees.

The private voice of psychology counters workplace discrimination not by punishment but by enhancing empathy. This is accomplished by ramping up training efforts to meet higher standards, encouraging employee reeducation, and expanding opportunities for rehabilitation.

We are a nation in misalignment. Eliminating sexual harassment in the current climate requires that we integrate the public and private voices of *all* employees—not just those who harass or become harassed—to build a cultural consensus that helps prevent a hostile work environment. The ultimate goal of Title VII law is to become obsolete so that employees do not need to monitor themselves at all. Their spontaneous actions and interactions will be consistent with the ideal.

Preventing Racial Harassment

Sylvan felt uneasy. . . . After working a quarter century of overtime and double shifts, he was forced to take disability leave after an injury. He did not think that he would be able to adjust to the slower pace of life in the few months it took him to fully recover.

But Sylvan surprised himself and proved to be a better patient than he thought he would be. For the first time in his adult years, he had the opportunity to step back from the daily grind and consider his situation at work. He didn't like what he saw.

He had been under a lot of pressure for a long time. Sylvan worked his way up the ranks to foreman in a major telecommunications company. He was the only African-American supervisor within the company. Sylvan believed that he had to succeed not only for himself, but also to set an example for the other African Americans who would come after him.

Sylvan assumed this responsibility as supervisor with quiet dignity, although there were plenty of days he wished he still was one of the guys. At least they had each other. As a supervisor, Sylvan missed the camaraderie of his pals but was never completely accepted by the other supervisors. Sylvan was in a class of his own.

Worse, there were even some occasions when he was asked by the boss to directly participate in the unfair treatment of the men. Sylvan's accident came on the tail of one of those trying times. The boss wanted to promote his favorites and bypass the

African-American employees. Behind closed doors, he asked Sylvan to help get around the regulations. Sylvan refused to help.

Sylvan was laid up on disability before he had a chance to discover what the repercussions would be. Today he would find out. Sylvan was apprehensive about returning to the plant because he had heard that the boss proceeded with the promotions and there was an undercurrent of deep resentment among the men. Sylvan was caught between an angry boss, who felt betrayed by him, and disappointed workers, who felt he had let them down.

Sylvan was greeted by a "gift" that was placed carefully atop the post next to his desk. From afar, it looked like some equipment that had been accidentally left behind by a worker in a hurry to pack up and go home on a Friday afternoon. As Sylvan drew closer, however, he realized that this was no piece of equipment.

It was a piece of rope. Sylvan stopped dead in his tracks. No black man could miss the message of the back-to-work present. It was a hangman's noose, wrapped around the neck of the stanchion.

Suspended in the moment, Sylvan responded to the overwhelming threat he perceived in the situation. He moved slowly and deliberately, visually scanning the room in order to discern even the smallest change in posture or expression of his coworkers that might be a clue to the identity of the hangman.

Sylvan could feel the presence of the harasser in the open space. He was acutely aware of his coworkers looking at him as he looked at them, their heads bent to avoid making eye contact. Through stolen glimpses, they waited to see his reaction to the hangman's noose.

No one stepped forward. Sylvan could hear the silence in the room. He paused, but only for a moment. Then he solemnly pulled his chair over toward the post, stepped up, and took down the piece of rope. On his descent, people began to move about, like statues breathing in life. It was back to "business as usual."

Sylvan reported the incident of the hangman's noose to his boss and later filed a complaint of racial harassment with human resources. The officer initiated an investigation and questioned the employees whom Sylvan identified as having been in the room when he arrived. There were eight in all.

Of those interviewed, six did not think the rope was a noose, but a loose coil that might have been carelessly left behind after completing a worksite. The other two employees were unsure of what the rope meant. The investigation ended without reaching a definitive conclusion.

Nothing happened after the first strike. No one came forward to offer information about the suspect rope. Three more weeks went by, and still nothing. On the following Monday morning, two fresh nooses mysteriously appeared on company property. One was on the back of a utility truck, dangling in a conspicuous spot, and the second was draped in a highly visible area in the commons, where employees congregated for breaks and open meetings.

This time, no one took the nooses down. The Phantom contemplated coming out from behind the shadows. He was pretty sure some of his buddies already knew who he was.

The Challenge

It is hard to believe that incidents like this still occur in the United States today, but the hangman's noose is one of the more recent symbols used by harassers against African-American employees to intimidate them on the job. The EEOC has several dozen hostile work environment cases that involve this menacing gesture.

The case of the hangman's noose is also a good prototype for racial harassment in American industry for reasons beyond the EEOC statistics. The noose symbolizes the most virulent form of racism in our national history. It evokes painful images of the Ku Klux Klan, where the attacker hid "under the hood" to evade punishment or prosecution by the law for crimes against blacks.

Correspondingly, in the workplace, many of the cases of

racial harassment on record also involve silent stalkers who hide their enmity and their identity behind the noose or similar symbols. Against the backdrop of these veiled hostilities, American workers have acquired a strong public voice prohibiting racial discrimination, based on decades of affirmative action and diversity training in the workplace.

Race is in its "old age" compared with some of the more recent employee groups to come under the umbrella of Title VII. It is the granddaddy of protected categories. Accordingly, learning from the experience of race will help us to know what to expect with the newer arrivals.

We propose that there is a natural life cycle of the protected class that unfolds as the employees included in it are progressively assimilated into the mainstream culture of the work force. It occurs in stages that are ordered and predictable.

The law demands a change first in the public voice. It prohibits employers and employees from discrimination against members in the protected class. This does not change much inside the minds and hearts of workers, but requires of them at least superficial compliance to the letter of the law. Racial name-calling, bullying, slurring, and stereotyping have declined significantly as the public voice has gained in strength.

The next phase of the struggle is to change the private voice. It is the spirit of the law, and it varies from person to person. Employees fine-tune their inner beliefs at their own pace, some more readily than others. As the struggle to end racial discrimination progresses, the workplace becomes more mixed up with private voices that all sing in different keys. There is no harmony.

In one section of the choir are those workers, growing in number, who are successful in internalizing the public voice of the law as their own. They have little trouble in alignment and do not need external monitoring or control.

In the opposite section are workers who hold on to the old ways. They defend their perceptions with stubborn tenacity.

Though they are forced into silence by the law, waves of pressure from a changing culture deepen the rift between them and their coworkers.

Not even a strong public voice can withstand the undertow of divergent private voices. This is especially true if the rogue private voices are many in number or belong to employees who have powerful positions in the company.

Leadership plays a vital role in reconciling these normal differences in the rate of employee change. In the absence of such reconciliation, coworkers degenerate into an "us-versus-them" mentality—bad for business, in general, but a virtual hotbed for hostile work environment racial harassment outbreaks.

Though companies vary in how they master the midlife crisis of differing private voices, the endpoint of the process is always the same. There is social change. Eventually the diverse private voices come into alignment with the predominant public voice. The life cycle completes its course when the majority of employees internalize the law. Workers monitor themselves, and the group monitors those few who cannot.

Laws that mandate workplace behavior are meant to become obsolete once they have been internalized and accepted by the public. We are not there yet for racial harassment. Many American workers still harbor inner perceptions about race and racial differences that are not in alignment with the laws of the workplace. While a stern national conscience has all but squelched their public voices, continuing incidents of racial harassment testify to the ongoing breakthrough of their private voices.

The law provides a structure and an incentive to change the public voice. We have been less systematic as a nation in finding a uniform way to change the private voice. Employers have not had a concise tool kit to realign employee perception.

The proof?

Racial harassment is still the second most frequent type of hostile work environment complaint brought before the

EEOC, after sexual harassment. It is not only rogue employees who end up in court as targets in race discrimination lawsuits, but also major corporations such as Texaco and Coca-Cola, employers with track records in diversity training and affirmative action programs.

We need to understand the relationship between a relatively overdeveloped public voice and a disparate private voice in these companies. What do you do when the company is doing everything right procedurally but racial harassment occurs anyway? How do managers explicitly monitor and intervene when the private voices of some employees undermine the employer's public commitment?

Manager's Definition of Racial Harassment

In this panoply of change, there are some things that are always the same. Looking at the simple maxim we apply to all forms of hostile work environment harassment—racial and otherwise—the harassment *complaint* should not be confused with the harassment *problem*.

When hostile work environment racial harassment occurs, it is always a case of "more than meets the eye." The racial harassment incident or complaint is symptomatic of a deeper problem in the organization. Prevention is therefore always a matter of discovering where the true problem lies so that the harassment symptom can abate. The important question for the manager is, *who* in the organization is responsible for *what* part of the hostile work environment racial harassment?

In most corporations, human resources (or another assigned agent) records, investigates, and corrects racial harassment *complaints*. HR oversees the employer's public voice: its antiharassment policy and complaint procedure. There are few employees in the United States today who do not clearly know the public voice on racial harassment. As a culture, we have much exposure, beginning in childhood, to the dos and don'ts of racial decorum.

The private voice is more difficult to monitor. It is what employees really think and feel, sometimes below their level of awareness, but what they express indirectly in their work relationships. The employer has no direct contact with the private voice. It falls to managers to oversee its harmony with the public voice in the day-to-day interactions among the employees they supervise.

The manager's definition of racial harassment is therefore different from that of human resources. HR has a *procedural* definition of racial harassment. It is based on compliance to policy and law. The manager has an *interpersonal* definition of racial harassment. It is based on how employees treat one another. When the two are not in alignment, the risk of an employee incident increases.

Using the manager's definition, two conditions must be met for racial harassment to occur:

1. The public and private voices of the victim are in misalignment.
2. The public and private voices of the harasser are in misalignment.

To prevent racial harassment, therefore, the proactive manager aligns the public and private voices of all parties involved in the harassment crisis.

There is one important way in which racial harassment is different from other types of hostile work environment harassment. Because of a strongly censuring public voice, accusations of racial harassment evoke great apprehension. Managers fear the recrimination that could come if they are perceived by their employees as taking sides, especially in companies where there is sharp divisiveness below the surface. A racial harassment complaint can break open a hornet's nest of hidden resentments that managers may wish to avoid.

We would advise managers to do otherwise. Positive change in companies as large as Texaco or Coca-Cola is testimony to what can be accomplished by employees, including managers, when they do not stand back—even in cases in which the racial discrimination alleged is systemic and adversely affects thousands of workers.

Manager's Tool Kit

We will give the manager a seven-step tool kit to learn how to identify critical misalignments between the public and private voices that leave the company vulnerable to hostile work environment racial harassment. These tools prevent such problems from erupting, or contain an existing problem before it grows bigger. If a manager learns about an incident, we recommend using these steps to realign the perceptions of the accuser and the accused in relation to the organization.

Step 1. Align the Public and Private Voices of the Accuser

Follow These Steps to Accomplish Step 1

To bring greater alignment of the public and private voices of the accuser, we recommend that the manager:

- Reassure the accuser that racial harassment is not tolerated in the company. This does not interfere with the role of human resources. You are not making a judgment about the particular incident, only asserting that the company policy is for the protection of *all* employees.
- Reassure the accuser that racial harassment behavior is one of the inappropriate ways some workers express personal hostility and frustration. Some employees are perceived as easy targets who won't or can't fight back. You are not a counselor; you are only a support who acknowledges that the harassment problem may be bigger than the harassment complaint.
- Reassure the accuser that he or she is not alone.

When the manager provides this support, accusers can still be mistrustful (the manager could be the harasser's friend) or angry (why didn't the manager protect me in the first place?). Supervisors must assure the accuser, *I am going to try to make this place safe for you.*

In the first stage of hostile work environment racial harassment, the misalignment is between the public and private voices of the employee accuser. There are many scenarios of racial harassment that we can imagine, but most of the time, the accuser knows that the treatment that is received "feels wrong." With the strength of law behind this employee, what stops him or her from putting an end to the situation, and what can the manager do to help?

Sylvan is a good example of how, even in cases that feel unambiguously hostile to the victim, the public and private voices of the victim still part ways.

Let us start with the public voice.

Sylvan's public voice is highly principled and assertive. He takes the responsibility of foreman seriously. He sees it as his job to set an example for the workers he supervises and to protect the shop against racial harassment. Sylvan expresses his public voice loud and clear. He takes down the hangman's noose and files a formal charge of harassment.

The public voice of the victim says, "Protect the company's standard."

Like many racial harassment victims today, Sylvan knows the law, he knows his civil rights, and he knows his work responsibilities. His public voice is above reproach.

But his private voice pulls him in another direction.

Racial harassment catapults its victims into a class by themselves. Singled out as the target of hostility, victims are separated from their coworkers. They are made visible in a way that is extremely uncomfortable and threatening. Victims are robbed of the safety and anonymity of the group.

Sylvan's public voice protects himself and his coworkers— and thus the company—by taking an affirmative stand and removing the suspect noose. But this action does nothing to assuage inner concerns. He feels unprotected and unsafe in the work environment. The public voice does not have the power to make the victim feel secure. Something more is needed.

The private voice of the victim says, "Protect yourself."

The splitting of public and private voices of victims of racial harassment is quite common. The alienation they experience is compounded when the hostility is veiled or when the identity of the harasser is concealed. Unfortunately, both of these conditions are common in racial harassment cases because the harasser is not able to openly engage in misconduct.

When is a rope a noose?

It is hard for racial harassment victims to know how to react when an incident feels worse than it looks. If you complain, will you lose what you have worked so hard to gain on the job? What if you are overreacting? Victims harbor these thoughts.

Proactive managers can accomplish a great deal at this stage of the problem if they appreciate that even subtle acts of racial hostility have a profound impact on the victim. Supervisors are not responsible for making judgments about racial harassment incidents. Nor should they talk to accusers about the facts of the matter, unless explicitly instructed to do so by the employer.

But managers are responsible for exploring with victims what the conflicts are that contribute to the racial harassment problem. Are there racial inequities that fueled the incident? Are there other changes in the company that are disruptive to the employees and that are surfacing in the form of racial harassment? Why are racial resentments surfacing now?

The manager's goal is twofold. First, reassure the employee that he or she is not alone and that the supervisor is available if further incidents occur. This is the manager's protective role. And second, the supervisor listens to the private voice of the victim to discern what the sources of the harassment problem are. When appropriate, corrections in the department are made.

Any act of racial harassment is a serious red flag that there is an employee problem in the organization. The proactive manager's intervention at this time, therefore, may not only help the victim, but also prevent an employee episode from becoming a departmental crisis.

Step 2. Align the Public and Private Voices of the Accused

Follow These Steps to Accomplish Step 2

To bring greater alignment of the public and private voices of the accused, we recommend that the manager meet with the employee and his or her coworkers and:

- Explain that racial harassment is not tolerated in the company. Avoid talking about the actual incident or naming names. Investigating the harassment complaint is the job of human resources. Your goal is to reassure all parties that you are there to protect the employees in the department.
- Explain that racial harassment behavior is one of the inappropriate ways some workers express personal hostility and frustration. Explore with the harasser what these frustrations are. Assure your employees that you are aware that the harassment problem may be bigger than the harassment complaint.
- Explain how *no one* is safe unless *everyone* is safe. Victims are never alone.

When the manager provides this support, the harasser is indirectly put on notice, and the natural healing power of the group is summoned to protect all workers. The victim is less alienated, and the harasser is discouraged from doing more damage. If you find it difficult to follow this step, pay close attention to steps 3 and 4 and learn why.

The accused employee in this case is a phantom harasser, if indeed the rope was meant to be a hangman's noose in the first place. How strong a position should a manager take about an act of questionable intent, committed by an actor of unknown identity?

Human resources struggled with this same question in the vignette. The officer did not know if the coil was initially *intended* to be a symbol of racism and tried to establish the fact pattern based on the observations of the employees who were present on the scene. The majority said, "No, it was a coil!"

Sylvan said, "Yes, it was a noose!" Should we take a vote to decide if this is racial harassment?

We may wonder what is going on in a case like this. Everybody involved knows the law.

The harasser's public voice says, "Racial harassment is wrong."

The racial harasser also knows that harassment is wrong. We have not encountered any cases, nor is it easy to imagine one, in which a racial harasser does not know the public voice of the law. The problem lies elsewhere.

The coil is a perfect foil for the harasser's private voice:

The harasser's private voice says, "Just don't get caught."

The noose is a veiled message. What does it convey about the sender?

Racial harassers are often disgruntled employees with numerous woes about life on the job. Racial differences become the funnel for these discontents. The harassment is an expression of hostility and frustration. Accused employees usually do not feel they are getting their just rewards on the job, and they perceive the victim as a safe target for indignities felt by the private voice.

The public and private voices do an interesting parley with each other in racial harassment. Social censure comes along with the territory of a strong public voice. Harassment on the basis of race is unequivocally prohibited. This drives the workings of the private voice underground. Thus, in one way, the public voice inhibits racial harassment.

But censure also inadvertently fuels the private voice. Remember that the harasser is usually an employee who feels quite powerless to change his or her personal problems or patterns at work. The challenge of "not getting caught" is empowering to harassers. Veiled harassment gestures heighten the victim's intimidation. And because they are done anonymously, they tie the supervisor's hands. The harasser feels an inflated sense of control.

The first job of the manager therefore is to demystify and defuse the harasser's private voice.

The proactive manager can do this whether or not the identity of the racial harasser is known. In the worst-case scenario, even when the supervisor has no *direct* access to the employee behind the racial harassment act, numerous pathways of *indirect* access to the accused are still open for action.

In the case of a phantom harasser, we recommend the proactive manager follow the steps outlined below. These address the private voice and make sure this employee knows that his or her messages are not unnoticed.

Supervisors can have informal discussions with employees, either in small groups or one-on-one, to solicit their reactions when a racial harassment incident occurs. The goal is to build a strong protective alliance with each employee in the department so that an atmosphere of safety is restored. This sends a powerful message to the accused that he or she, and not the victim, is isolated in the department.

The proactive manager can also invite human resources and executive leaders to talk to employees in the department directly about the incident and reinforce the employer's position against racial intimidation and harassment. This demonstrates the commitment of leadership to stand behind its policy. The employer's presence also signals a powerful message to the accused that racial harassment is not tolerated.

If the identity of the harasser *is* known, we recommend that the proactive manager meet with the employee. It is not the manager's job to investigate the harassment incident or to reach a verdict about culpability. Human resources conducts the formal investigation. But it is the supervisor's job to explore with the harasser what conflicts he or she may be experiencing that are intensifying the harassment problem. These employees often believe that their hostility against the victim is justified, even if the harassment acts are not. When harassers separate their justifications from their actions in this way, they excuse themselves from responsibility.

The supervisor helps the accused employee clarify this distinction. While harassment behavior is never excused, if there is legitimate cause for the harasser's discontent, the supervisor makes an appropriate effort to correct the problem in the department and thereby defuse continued misdirection of hostility. If there is nothing in the work environment that is fueling the racial harassment, the supervisor should carefully monitor the harasser's ongoing behavior, document these observations, and report to human resources or another assigned agent.

The manager may be the only person who has access to the racial harasser to make these important observations. This reduces the chance of the harassment continuing or even escalating.

Step 3. Align the Public and Private Voices of the Manager about the Victim

Follow These Steps to Accomplish Step 3

To bring greater alignment of your public and private voices about the victim, we recommend that you:

- Explore your feelings about potential retaliation if you come forward and acknowledge the victim's experience. Do you believe you have your employer's full support?
- Explore your feelings about the harassment incident and ask yourself if you are able to be an impartial supervisor. Be aware that it is common for people to blame the victim when harassment occurs. This means we look for a "reason" why it happened to a particular employee. We do this when the harassment makes us feel very uncomfortable.
- Seek the help of a trusted friend or colleague to talk to about these issues to make sure that you are not blind to some bias that could keep you from helping and supporting the victim.

When managers take stock of their own feeling of security in the organization and of their personal reactions to racial harassment, they are better able to help victims. Getting a second opinion on your perception is good prevention. It protects you and the victim.

When management does not respond proactively to the harassment problem, racial hostility intensifies. The harasser is encouraged by the implicit green light he or she receives from a passive employer. Rumors start to spread, and it is easy to imagine that underground factions form in the organization. This spells disaster for the racial harassment victim, whose isolation and alienation increase.

These are serious consequences to the department when the manager does not respond to the harassment problem. From years of counseling employers and consulting to industry, however, we learned that this is not an unusual reaction. Managers also have a public and private voice, and when they are not in alignment, their ability to supervise racial harassment victims is compromised.

When we listen to supervisors, we learn that one of the greatest deterrents to using knowledge in the public voice to help harassment victims comes from the conflicting messages of their private voices. While it is the job of supervisors to advocate for all of the workers they supervise, they have a special task when it comes to racial harassment victims.

Supervisors are sandwiched between the employer, whose interests they serve, and employees, whom they are entrusted to protect. When the employer is sincere in its commitment to zero tolerance for racial harassment, it is easier for the managers to oversee compliance to company policy among the employees. The managers are not in conflict about their supervisory responsibilities.

Unfortunately, there are still many companies in which the employer's private voice is weak or ambivalent about enforcing antiharassment policy. When the employer is not firm in word and deed, the manager is caught in the middle. Supervisors may want to respond empathically to the racial harassment victim, but they are also getting a message from the employer to minimize or ignore the problem.

This creates a state of conflict for the supervisor, who cannot be expected to minimize the harassment situation and also empathize with the victim. In trying to "ride two horses," the managers succeed in doing neither. Psychologically, when the company abandons the victim, it also abandons the supervisor. The employer's denial has a profound impact on the manager, not just on the harassment victim.

Sometimes the pressure on managers is too great, and they buckle.

When the manager's public voice colludes with the employer's private voice, the racial harassment problem escalates.

Here is how it works. If the managers' fear of retaliation by the employer for sticking their neck out is strong enough, the managers will follow the employer's lead and also abandon the victim.

What does it look like when supervisors abandon victims?

To lessen their internal conflict between the public and private voices, supervisors are prone to discount the negative intentions of the harasser or minimize the severity of the harassment experienced. These perceptual adjustments are relatively easy to make when the harassment complaint is ambiguous or is based only on the interpretation of the accuser.

What happens to the department when supervisors abandon victims?

The manager's denial cascades down to coworkers. It is a good bet that this is precisely what enabled six of the eight employees in the case study at the beginning of the chapter to report to human resources that the rope was a coil and not a noose. Did they really believe their own statements? We cannot say for sure. But based on our research, employees will alter their public voice to avoid retaliation, though this does not alter their private beliefs. This last point is critical, because it carries harsh implications for managers.

What happens to the supervisors themselves when they abandon victims?

Sadly, not only do misaligned supervisors lose empathy for racial harassment victims, but they also lose the trust of the other employees in the department. Though workers may not say anything, they are very disappointed in this manager. Deep inside, employees fear that the manager could abandon them just as he or she did the harassed employee.

It is important for managers to know that conflicted reactions to racial harassment victims are normal, especially if the employer is not strongly committed to its antiharassment policy in word and deed. This places the manager in a tight squeeze.

It is helpful for supervisors to talk to a trusted person in the organization about their reactions, especially if they are supervising a harassed employee. It is also helpful to get concrete guidance from the employer on how to assist in the recovery process. The needed skills do not automatically come with the territory of supervisor. Do not be reluctant to ask for support.

Step 4. Align the Public and Private Voices of the Manager about the Harasser

---

Follow These Steps to Accomplish Step 4

To bring greater alignment of your public and private voices about the harasser, we recommend that you:

- Explore your feelings about potential retaliation if you come forward and acknowledge the harassment occurred. Are you afraid of retaliation by your employer for upsetting the apple-cart over a problem the company wants to ignore?
- Explore your feelings about the harasser and ask yourself if you are able to be an impartial supervisor. Be aware that it is common for managers to fear becoming the harasser's next victim, especially when the employer ignores the problem.
- Seek the help of a trusted friend or colleague to talk to about these issues to make sure that you are not blind to some bias that could get in the way of your helping the harasser and preventing future harassment episodes.

When managers take stock of their own sense of vulnerability, they are in a better position to supervise the racial harasser with empathy and impartiality. Because this can be a very difficult task, we advise all managers to get a second opinion on their perceptions. It protects you and the accused.

Nowhere is it more important for the manager to be in good alignment than when addressing the supervisory needs of an employee accused of racial harassment. Prevention is most directly served by the effective monitoring of this employee. It is therefore important for managers to consider the common roadblocks that prevent them from successfully engaging the racial harasser in an effort to either correct offensive behavior or make the appropriate referral to human resources for disciplinary action.

There are two common obstacles we see that stop managers from using or developing their skills to align the public and private voices of accused employees. First, many supervisors are intimidated by the harassers and have not been trained in how to supervise these individuals. These managers should ask their employer for concrete guidance.

The second obstacle is more difficult to overcome. Just as we saw in the case of the victim, the "invisible hand" of the employer can inhibit the manager from helping rehabilitate the harasser when the employer fails to give the manager a clear signal to end the racial harassment. When this happens, managers are caught in a bind.

Just as with victims, managers' public voices advise them *not* to ignore the interpersonal problems of the harasser. But their private voices caution that the employer's denial is an implied demand that they too should "make the problem go away."

When the manager's public voice colludes with the employer's private voice, the manager becomes the harasser's next victim.

Here is how it works. If fear of retaliation by the employer for exposing the problem the employer wants to whisk away is strong enough, managers also ignore the harasser.

• What does it look like when supervisors ignore harassers?

As we have seen, ignoring the problem neither makes it go away nor helps the manager. The harasser gains the upper hand and continues on a course of intimidation. A subtle game of blackmail begins below the table, between the harasser and the manager. The harasser pushes the envelope to see how far he or she can go. The manager gets entrapped in his or her own web of denial.

• What happens to the department when supervisors ignore harassers?

The harasser makes supervisors "pay double" for collusion with the boss. The supervisors lose all authority to confront the harassment problem, and they also lose the respect and cooperation of the other employees in the department, who see what is going on. Hiding behind the employer's misalignment is a lose-lose proposition for the manager.

• What happens to supervisors themselves when they ignore harassers?

Anger mounts as they react to the subtle but constant manipulation of the harasser. It is a good bet that eventually the manager's pent-up frustration will bubble to the surface. Who better a target than the harasser, who has started all the trouble in the first place? We find that managers give up on racial harassers, see them as hopeless, ignore them, or react punitively to them. These are all forms of displaced hostility that cause managers to lose empathy for the accused employee.

It is not the job of the supervisor to pass judgment on the racial harasser. What these employees need from the supervisor is clear, straightforward, and unbiased feedback on workplace behavior so the public and private voices can be brought into alignment. Managers are often the only ones in the organization who are in a position to give accused harassers a second chance to correct misalignments, while also protecting the work environment. It is unfortunate when managers surrender this special opportunity because they have lost empathy in this triangle of misalignment.

It is important for managers to talk to a trusted person in the organization about their reactions to the employees they supervise in relation to the hostile environment racial harassment crisis. This gives them the time they need to sort out their own feelings of anger or frustration about the position they find themselves in and to free up their energies to deal effectively with the problem at hand.

Step 5. Align the Private Voices of the Victim and the Employer

---

Follow These Steps to Accomplish Step 5

To bring greater alignment of the private voices of the victim and the employer, we recommend that, as a manager, you:

- Make sure that you follow the company's antiharassment policy and report all known incidents of racial harassment. Under no circumstances is it to anyone's advantage to ignore a victim, especially one whom you also supervise.
- Make sure you follow up with victims who are harassed in your department. While you are not responsible for correcting the racial harassment incident, you are responsible to be on the watch for other manifestations of the harassment problem.
- Make sure you share your observations with your employer. Use the harassment incident to leverage improvements for the department. This helps the victim and ultimately the whole company.

When managers fulfill their function as intermediaries and communicate clearly to the victims of racial harassment and to their employer, they are safeguarding the company from further problems. No matter what your employer thinks *now*, later on you will be glad you did not relinquish your important role.

We come to the hardest part of the manager's job when dealing with racial harassment. This is closing the gaps between the harassment parties and the employer. Virtually every organization today has a policy against racial discrimination and harassment and a strong public voice that prohibits it. We have suggested that the private voice in some organizations is not always as strong, and this causes problems for managers, victims, and harassers.

The vignette at the beginning of the chapter presented a difficult but common dilemma. The manager is supervising an employee who believes he is being racially harassed and who acts in accordance to the antiharassment policy and files a complaint to the employer. But the harassment problem does not end.

Most real cases of racial harassment happen just this way. If we review court records, we inevitably discover a chain of errors, as one person's misperception of the harassment problem gives implicit consent to the next person in the chain of command, who acts on the same interpretation. Misjudgment compounds each step of the way, up to the courthouse steps.

It is not that these multiple participants—supervisors, human resource counselors, executives—do not "know better." Something stops them from "doing better" with what they know. What is it that enables this tragedy of errors to occur with such regularity, and what is the manager's responsibility in breaking the chain reaction?

When an employee is racially harassed, the manager is involved in a situation he or she neither created nor has the ultimate authority to correct.

Supervisors do not have control over the harasser or the employer, and yet they are responsible to act affirmatively on behalf of the victim. What a spot! When under this kind of pressure, a manager's ability to make decisions suffers.

This can be explained psychologically. We know from much experimental research that when ordinary people are put under strong pressure to defend a position they do not agree with, they will eventually come to believe their own defense. This phenomenon even has a name. It is called *cognitive dissonance*.

Similarly, when the employer puts pressure (directly or indirectly) on managers to minimize a victim's experience, the managers will unconsciously look selectively at the evidence that supports the employer's perception. It is not that managers want to contribute to the chain of command of poor decision making. Rather, their actions come from the need to reduce their own internal conflict in having participated in a decision they do not believe in.

These misperceptions and the decisions based on them prove to be particularly harmful to the victim of racial harassment and eventually to the whole company. We have already shown how collusion with the employer's private voice takes away from the manager's capacity to be an effective supervisor. Now we see how it can also stop managers from giving important feedback to the person in the company who most needs to know—the boss.

This is how we get a tragedy of errors. The effects of a manager's misaligned private and public voices and collusion with the employer's voice ripples up and down the organization. We have noted the critical position the supervisor occupies between the employer and the staff workers. Supervisors are intermediaries who keep the lines of communication open between the employer and staff workers. When the supervisors withhold important information from responsible authorities, prevention is impossible and harassment escalates.

What is it that managers who supervise racial harassment victims need to communicate to the employer?

It is your job to advocate for the best interests of all the workers you supervise—including racial harassment victims. It is especially important for the victim to know that you are bringing his or her concerns to the attention of executive management.

If problems in the department are uncovered in the course of the harassment investigation, use this as an opportunity. This is a good time to talk to your boss about the urgency of getting needed resources to correct these problems so that the underlying tensions diminish in your unit.

When a harassment victim can see positive change come about as a result of his or her painful experience, it boosts recovery in the best possible way.

Step 6. Align the Private Voices of the Harasser and the Employer

Follow These Steps to Accomplish Step 6

To bring greater alignment of the private voices of the harasser and the employer, we recommend that, as a manager, you:

- Make sure you follow the company's antiharassment policy and report all known incidents of racial harassment. Under no circumstances is it to anyone's advantage to ignore a harasser, especially one whom you also supervise.
- Make sure you follow up with harassers, especially if you are also their supervisor. While you are not responsible for correcting the racial harassment incident, you are responsible for potential hostility the harasser may display in your department and for preventing avoidable future harassment episodes.
- Make sure you share your observations with your employer. This protects you, the other employees in your department, and ultimately your employer.

When managers fulfill their function as intermediaries and communicate clearly to harassers and to their employers, they are safeguarding the company from further problems. No matter how your employer reacts *now*, you will be glad that you did not bury your head in the sand. You want to be a part of the solution, not a part of the problem, especially if the racial harassment reaches a crisis proportion.

The problem of correcting the misalignment of the public and private voices of the employer in relation to the harasser is similar to that of the victim. When there are misalignments, the risk of a continuing problem increases. But failing to give feedback to the employer about a potential harasser has even more serious consequences than ignoring a victim in the long-term outcome of the organization.

There is a corollary to the cognitive dissonance definition we used earlier to explain how supervisors reconcile their conflict between the employer's private voice telling them to ignore the problem and their duty to support the victims of the racial harassment. This corollary often operates on an unconscious level, and it is counter to intuition. The more a supervisor feels pressured internally into adopting the employer's position when the supervisor does not agree with it, the more strongly the supervisor will externally defend it.

Applying this to supervisors in their perceptions of racial harassers, we begin to understand the common reaction of disbelief we have when reading the proceedings of real court cases. We see how it happens that the accusations about the behavior of racial harassers that are so glaring under the microscope of the court could have seemed so ambiguous or even benign when they occurred at work.

When the victim of the racial harassment is strong enough and pushes back against the company, the walls of collusion of the supervisor, employer, and harasser come tumbling down, and the private voices of all the parties are exposed. Managers do not want to find themselves in this position.

When an employee is accused of racial harassment, the manager is responsible for explicitly acknowledging the problem even if the employer implicitly ignores it.

The proactive supervisor really has no choice.

What are some of the things supervisors can do to close the gap between the harasser's private voice and that of the employer? They can evaluate the interpersonal skills of the harasser generally, outside of the harassment complaint, and report back to the employer. This is vital information for the company.

Employers make decisions about the rehabilitation status of accused racial harassers. But they often make these decisions with very little direct information. Some racial harassers can be helped, though others are best terminated. Even then, however, reliable feedback from the supervisor helps the employer make a fair decision that also reduces the risk of a counterlawsuit for wrongful termination if the racial harasser strikes again.

As logical as all this sounds, in a surprising number of cases, managers collude with their employer and ignore the hostile environment racial harassment problem. This has tragic consequences for all parties. It is our turn to "come out from behind the noose." The vignette described in the beginning of this chapter is based on a true event (though the description of Sylvan's inner experience is fictitious). The actual outcome of the racial harassment problem in that case?

A class-action lawsuit was filed against the corporation.

- Sylvan independently sued the company for wrongful termination and race discrimination after his second request for short-term medical disability was denied. He alleged unfair treatment by his employer based on race, stating more favorable accommodations were given to nonminority injured employees. Sylvan cited the noose incidents as evidence of the employer's tolerance for racial discrimination.
- Several other nooses were discovered in the plant. On investigation, it was learned that five supervisors and a company president saw the nooses, which hung in the same prominent location for a period of over two years. Other African-American employees joined Sylvan's lawsuit and alleged that their employer tacitly approved a workplace rife with racial discrimination and harassment.
- The employer defended its conduct by stating that the nooses were probably "in poor taste" but not intended to "hurt anyone."
- The African-American employees asserted that they did not complain about the hangman's nooses in all that time because they feared being labeled as "troublemakers" and losing their jobs.

In this class-action lawsuit, the employer's private voice was on trial.

Step 7. Provide Employee Training

The last step for the proactive manager is to bring together all levels of the organization in one united gesture to align the public and private voices of all employees. We suggest that training in racial harassment prevention should be a regular part of any employer's commitment to provide a workplace that is free of racial hostility and intimidation.

It is important to include all employees and not just the line staff. When workers see the participation of executives, professionals, managers, and nonsupervisory employees, it underscores the employer's sincerity. Workers need to know that the company's commitment goes beyond the piece of paper the policy is written on. They also need to be assured that if an incident occurs, the employer will live up to its policy commitment in responding appropriately.

Throughout this chapter, we have emphasized the special ways that managers can contribute to the alignment of the public and private voices to prevent racial harassment. We have argued that they may even need to inch forward when the employer backs away. This is a challenge for any supervisor, especially in companies where the employer's private voice is giving mixed signals.

Earlier in this chapter we discussed the premise that we are a nation in transition. Many workers have successfully internalized the federal standards prohibiting racial discrimination as their own. These employees are already in good alignment with the employer's policy. But we still have gaps, and these erupt in the form of hostile environment racial harassment, which has broad impact on the whole organization.

Training is the final step the proactive manager can take to help close the gaps, not only between the public and private voices of the harassment partners, but also among all employees. Cultural consensus is the goal of preventive training. It is what ultimately eradicates cultural bias, including all forms of racial harassment.

Preventing Disability
Harassment

Carmel was employed as a medical assistant by a prominent physician's group located in the southern United States. She relayed to her supervisor and to her former coworker and friend that she is HIV-positive. Carmel was surprised when her former friend stopped socializing with her at work, intercepted and eavesdropped on her personal telephone calls, and began to hover around her desk. Carmel also noticed changes in the way the president of the company interacted with her. He would go to great pains to circumvent her office and avoided ordinary physical contact with her, such as refusing to shake her hand in a routine greeting gesture.

Carmel's problems did not stop here. Soon she was required by her employer to take random drug tests to an excessive degree. Within one month of her disclosure of her medical condition, she was "written up" and placed on 90-day probation, with no prior record of similar performance problems. After the first probation period ended, she was immediately placed on second 90-day probation. Tensions between her and her supervisors increased and when she complained, she was accused of being a complainer. Eventually Carmel was terminated from employment.

Carmel filed a lawsuit against her employer alleging that she was terminated because of her disability, and that she was subjected to "harassing" conduct with the intention of forcing her out of her job. A jury found that her disability was not a motivating factor in her employer's decision to fire her, but

*that she was subjected to disability-based harassment that cre-
ated a hostile work environment.*

The Challenge

Employees with disabilities are protected against discrimination and harassment in the workplace. Federal law defines disability broadly. It applies to any person who has a mental or
physical impairment that substantially limits one or more major life activities. These include walking, standing, seeing, hearing, reasoning, and other functional capacities relating to work.

Inclusion in the protected category is determined on a
case-by-case basis. Sensory deficits, such as blindness or deafness, and most major diseases that affect motor skills are
clearly within the definition. More difficult to determine are
conditions like back injuries, learning disabilities, alcoholism,
or psychiatric disorders.

The right to freedom from workplace discrimination is
guaranteed to disabled people through the Americans with
Disabilities Act of 1990 (ADA). The job application process,
working conditions, and the right to equal employment benefits are directly addressed by law to prohibit discrimination
against otherwise qualified individuals. Title VII extends these
protections, probating harassment on the basis of disability.

What is the implication for the employer?

Managers need to be more concerned than ever before
about hostile environment harassment of workers with disabilities. Complicating the matter, it is not only obvious disabilities that managers need to be mindful of, but a host of
other conditions like alcoholism or depression, which are
quite common among the general population and therefore
also common in the workplace.

Unlike other classes of protected employees, the parameters for inclusion of disabled employees are broad and unsta-
ble. Employees can come in and out from under the umbrella of the ADA, due to changing need and life circumstance.
What accounts for the fluid boundaries of this group?

In some cases, medical advances improve the life expec-
tancy of individuals with diseases such as AIDS or cancer, and

employees who were not able to sustain work in the past are now in the work force. In other cases, changes in technology create new conditions such as stress injuries that challenge traditional thinking about what is a disability. Also, as we learn more about brain functioning, a physical basis of certain psychiatric and learning conditions justifies their inclusion as work-related disabilities.

The constancy of change gives disabled employees a special status among the categories of workers protected by federal law. There is no one profile of an employee who typifies the whole group. Though this can be confusing to managers, the diversity of disabilities gives us a special opportunity to study the underpinnings of harassment more closely, as we watch the evolution of the public and private voice for each distinct disability type.

We will look first at how the wide range of disabilities affects the evolution of the collective public voice, which informs the social conscience. Because of the diversity of worker impairments, a consistent public voice has been slow to develop. This means that employees may not know what to think about disabled coworkers. Limited exposure to them has resulted in few opportunities to form accurate impressions. The public voice suffers from impoverished education.

In the absence of concrete information about the disabled person, the employee's public voice is forced to come to its own conclusion using the only resource it has available. This is direct observation. We discover that what affects our public voice is not so much the *actual* disability of the worker in question, but the *perceived* disability.

This is an intriguing proposition. What employees think about the disabled person is based not on facts, but on the perception of facts. This is fertile ground for prejudice and stereotyping. Accordingly, based only on the power of direct observation, the public voice distinguishes two broad groups of employees with disabilities, those with visible and those with invisible differences.

Disabled employees with visible differences include individuals whose impairments are immediately recognizable by visual inspection, so much so that not even federal law requires them to document their condition. Employees with cognitive, sensory, or motor limitations due to blindness, deafness, muteness, multiple sclerosis, mental retardation, amputation, or cerebral palsy are examples of this group.

The second group includes disabled employees with impairments that also have a physical basis, though it is "invisible" to surface inspection. Employees with cognitive, sensory, or motor limitations due to learning disabilities, depression, back injury, alcoholism, or HIV virus are examples of this group.

The distinction between visible and invisible impairments is not meaningful in terms of the employee's actual ability to perform work. It is, however, important when considering the perception of the employee's ability to work. This is a critical point, because the public voice grows directly out of these surface perceptions and misperceptions.

In the absence of public education or prior exposure, employees form impressions about the disabled person using only their common sense. They perceive the most obviously impaired workers as the most deserving of protection and accommodation in the workplace. Hence employees with visible disabilities naturally evoke the loudest public voice.

This may seem on the surface to be *reasonable*, but is it?

No! The truth is counter to intuition. The need for accommodation does not depend on the actual or perceived severity of the employee's impairment. It depends on the overall *fit* of job requirements, employee abilities, and coping capacities in relation to the impairment. Thus "smaller" or invisible impairments may have greater impact than "bigger" ones, and vice versa, depending on the person and the job situation.

A physical *impairment* only becomes a *handicap* when it stops individuals from performing work they *want* to do.

Nonetheless, we have a collective public voice that strongly censors any form of hostility against persons *perceived* as weak, injured, or not "whole." These are the visibly disabled. Taboos against hurting the helpless go back as far as biblical times.

The public voice, however, is not as strong a deterrent to harassment of individuals with invisible impairments. These employees may not even be perceived as disabled by their coworkers. This presents a special challenge to managers and employers who want to sustain a strong public voice that prohibits harassment of *all* impaired employees.

In the absence of a uniform public voice to guide employee thinking about disabled persons, the private voice has no steady mooring. This opens a second door of vulnerability to harassment. We discover that the private voice also forms in response to a chain of psychological reactions that ordinary people experience, again none of which have much to do with the worker's actual impairment. But they do predict who is at risk for disability harassment.

The chain reaction begins with a well-researched factor called the *social attractiveness* of the disability. It describes the range of tolerance ordinary people have to particular impairments. All disabilities are not created equal. The less "attractive" the impairment, the harsher and more stigmatizing the private voice.

Research teaches us that attractiveness is also based on certain predictable factors, again having less to do with the impairment itself than with the perception of the impairment. Both alcoholism and the HIV virus are examples of highly unattractive conditions that evoke a punitive private voice, compared with paraplegia or hearing impairment, for instance, both of which evoke coworker sympathy.

Surprisingly, the underlying perception that predicts social stigma is how the individual actually acquires the impairment, and not the physical characteristics or debility of the condition itself. If a disability is acquired accidentally, we are more forgiving of its victims. It is "not their fault." If the impairment is the result of a life choice, we blame the disabled person. This is how stigma and the private voice work.

Blaming the victim, as in the cases of employees with AIDS or alcoholism, for example, results in psychological distancing, which leads to a loss in empathy. This is a phenomenon of the private voice. If empathy is lost *and* there is not at least a strong public voice in operation, the risk for disability harassment is significant.

What is the status of hostile work environment disability harassment in the country today?

We have very few reported legal cases of harassment

against individuals with visible disabilities. This is presumably because of the impact of strong laws that prohibit it *and* a universal public voice that supports the law.

There is one caveat to this claim. Although disability *harassment* of employees with visible impairments is relatively uncommon, we do not dismiss the problem of *discrimination* against members of this group. There are still many cases pending against employers and public institutions for failing to provide physical accommodations to such employees and for denying them equal access to work opportunities.

The larger problem in the area of preventing hostile work environment disability harassment, however, is protecting employees whose impairments are *not* visible. This includes but is not limited to employees with AIDS or HIV virus, alcoholism, depression, and other psychiatric disorders and learning impairments—conditions that are not accepted by the ordinary worker as disabilities. The absence of an informed public voice to steady a highly charged private voice invites misalignment.

The prohibitions and penalties associated with the Americans with Disabilities Act impact the way people *act*. These prohibitions and penalties cannot reach to the private voice to change the way people *feel*. Proactive managers are challenged to integrate disabled employees in their departments, neither segregating them through unnecessary overprotection nor denying them deserved protection from discrimination and harassment.

Manager's Definition of Disability Harassment

Starting with the rule of thumb we apply to all forms of hostile work environment harassment, the harassment *complaint* should not be confused with the harassment *problem*.

When hostile work environment disability harassment occurs, it is symptomatic of a more pervasive problem with respect in the company. Passively allowing a disabled employee to be singled out for unfair treatment or harassment sounds an alarm to all workers that no one is safe.

If a disability harassment incident is a symptom of a deeper problem in the organization, prevention of future episodes is therefore a matter of discovering where the true problem lies. The important question for the manager is, *who* in the organization is responsible for *what* part of the hostile work environment disability harassment?

In most corporations, human resources (or another assigned agent) records, investigates, and corrects disability harassment *complaints*. HR oversees the employer's public voice: its antiharassment policy and complaint procedure.

The private voice is more difficult to monitor. It is what employees really think and feel, sometimes below their level of awareness, but what they express indirectly in their work relationships. The employer has no direct contact with the private voice of its employees. It falls to managers to oversee the harmony between the public and private voices in the day-to-day interactions among the employees they supervise.

The manager's definition of disability harassment is therefore different than that of human resources. The employer has a *procedural* definition, based on compliance to policy to policy and the Americans with Disabilities Act. The manager has an *interpersonal* definition of disability harassment. It is based on how employees treat one another. When the two are not in alignment, the risk of an employee incident increases.

Using the manager's definition, two conditions must be met for disability harassment to occur:

1. The public and private voices of the victim are in misalignment.
2. The public and private voices of the harasser are in misalignment.

To prevent disability harassment, therefore, the proactive manager aligns the public and private voices of all parties involved in the harassment crisis.

The manager must also bear in mind that disability harassment is unlike other forms of hostile work environment in one important respect. The target is usually in a class of his or her own in the workplace. In most cases, there are few, if any, other employees who share the special status of the disabled worker. This can make the experience of harassment all the more isolating and painful. The support of the manager takes on greater significance as he or she may be the only source of immediate relief to the harassed disabled person.

Manager's Tool Kit

We will give the manager a tool kit to learn how to identify critical misalignments between the public and private voices that leave the company vulnerable to disability harassment. These tools prevent such problems from erupting, or keep an existing problem from growing bigger. If a manager learns about an incident of hostile environment harassment of a disabled employee, we recommend using these seven steps to realign the perceptions of the accuser, the accused, and the organization.

Step 1. Align the Public and Private Voices of the Accuser

Follow These Steps to Accomplish Step 1

To bring greater alignment of the public and private voices of the accused, we recommend that the manager:

- Reassure the accuser that disability harassment is not tolerated in the company.
- Reassure the accuser that disability harassment is one of the inappropriate ways some coworkers express their personal hostility and frustration. Learn whether the accused feels respected and valued outside of the harassment incident.
- Reassure the accuser that he or she is not alone. Learn if there is a need to help the disabled employee assimilate into the broader work culture and reduce any feeling of personal alienation.

When the manager provides this support, the disabled accuser is less isolated in the harassment experience. He or she can still be angry (why didn't the manager protect me in the first place?) or mistrustful, but is safeguarded against continued scapegoating or being singled out. Supervisors must assure the employee *I am going to try to make this place safe for you.*

In the first stage of disability harassment, the misalignment is between the public and the private voices of the employee accuser. There are many possible sources of misalignment. Oftentimes, the public and private voices split because the social stereotype associated with the employee's disability contradicts the employee's perception of himself or herself. A disparity between the two creates a vulnerability to harassment.

How can the manager explore this? The first step in supervising disabled employees who allege hostile environment harassment is to find out how they perceive their work environment. Is it a case of disparity, where the employee believes he or she is being treated in a way that is inconsistent with prior experiences? The proactive manager probes the public and private voices of the disabled worker.

The public voice is not hard to discern. Most disabled employees today are fully versed in the impact of their impairments on job performance. Most know their needs and limitations. Accordingly, they recognize their differences and the role of the law in protecting them against undue discrimination and harassment.

The public voice of the disabled worker accepts protection against harassment as a fundamental right.

The private voice, however, can pull the disabled employee in another direction.

Disabled employees come to work with particular expectations about how they will be treated, based on prior life experiences. Workers with differences, especially visible impairments, usually have had years of exposure to the reactions of others to their disabilities. They have direct knowledge of how they are regarded and the prejudices (if any) they must overcome to gain acceptance.

The private voice translates past life experiences with others' perceptions of the disability to current expectations on the job.

If the disabled worker's prior experiences have been positive, or if he or she has been successful in overcoming the obstacles to acceptance, self-esteem is strong and the private voice anticipates a good outcome. This anticipation is in good alignment with a strong public voice that prohibits discrimination. Employees with this history do not readily become the targets of hostile work environment disability harassment.

In contrast, if the disabled worker's prior experiences have been negative, if the impairment is newly acquired, or if the employee's coping capacities have not been sufficient to overcome obstacles to success, self-esteem suffers. There is a mismatch between self-worth of the disabled employee (which may be high or low) and perceived value to others (which may also be high or low).

A disparity between these two perceptions increases the risk of an employee getting enmeshed in hostile environment exchanges at work. The direction of the mismatch predicts the type of harassment problem for which the employee is at risk. When self-worth is *higher* than perceived value to others, the disabled employee is oversensitive to perceived insult. When self-worth is *lower* than perceived value to others, the disabled employee is bent on self-defeat.

Both of these misaligned disabled employees are sitting ducks if a harasser comes their way.

The private voice of the disabled worker fears or anticipates exclusion or failure.

In the case of employees with visible impairments, negative anticipation may originate from having a disability with low "social attractiveness," such as mental retardation or physical deformity. In the case of employees with invisible impairments, it may be that the disability is one that evokes strong moral censure of coworkers, such as drug addiction. Or the disability may be one that the employee keeps secret, as in the case of the HIV virus.

It is important that the supervisor explore how employee accusers perceive coworkers' treatment of them in relation to their physical or mental differences. The manager has an opportunity to learn if the disabled employee has particular sensitivities based on past experiences that should be taken into account on the job.

Based on the manager's assessment, it may be beneficial for the supervisor to educate coworkers about the disability, or about the company's policy against harassment and discrimination of all disabilities. It is not the manager's job to reach a verdict about the harassment complaint, but to use it as an opportunity to learn if there is a more pervasive problem with acceptance of the disabled employee.

Based on years of experience consulting to industry, we have found that when disability harassment occurs, the employee often has a history of disappointment or has an impairment that falls into the category of "socially undesirable" and is therefore difficult to assimilate into the broader work culture.

Step 2. Align the Public and Private Voices of the Accused

Follow These Steps to Accomplish Step 2

To bring greater alignment of the public and private voices of the accused, we recommend that the manager meet with the employee and:

- Explain that disability harassment is not tolerated in the company. Avoid talking about the actual incident or making accusations. Investigating the harassment complaint is the job of human resources. Your goal is to make sure the harasser understands how decisions are made in the department regarding the fair treatment of all employees.
- Explain that disability harassment is one of the inappropriate ways workers express personal hostility or frustration with their jobs. Explore with the employee what discontent or perceived inequities are fueling the harassment problem.
- Explain how *no one* is safe unless *everyone* is safe. No victim is ever alone.

When the manager provides this support, the harasser is indirectly put on notice and the supervisor shields the disabled worker from further alienation and isolation. If you find it difficult to follow this step, pay close attention to steps 3 and 4.

The public and private voices of the accused employee are also in misalignment when hostile work environment disability harassment occurs. Research shows that these harassers usually experience strong reactions to what the disabled person *represents* to them, rather than to the disabled person as an individual.

Realignment therefore requires that the manager first understand the thinking of the disability harasser. It usually starts with misperceptions from the public voice. These are some common surface misrepresentations we often hear from disability harassers as justification for their actions.

The harasser may:

- Perceive reasonable accommodation to the disabled employee as unfair advantage
- Perceive association to the disabled employee as tarnishing his or her reputation
- Perceive proximity to the disabled employee as exposure to potential health or safety risks
- Perceive the disabled employee as a "favored pet" of the employer

This list is not exhaustive. Harassers have many misrepresentations of their disabled victims, most of which rest on fear, misinformation, and distortion.

The public voice of the disability harasser questions the validity of the victim's special status.

As noted earlier, problems of misalignment stemming from the public voice are less common in relation to employees with visible rather than invisible impairments. When an employee openly discriminates against a worker with *visible* disabilities, the situation is quite serious and the prognosis for rehabilitation less hopeful.

This is because it is not the public and private voices of the *harasser* that are in misalignment. They are in complete agreement and signal a green light to the harassment. The problem is that the harasser's public and private voices are in gross misalignment with the law. As already noted, this kind of disability harassment is fortunately rather uncommon today.

Misalignment of the harasser's public voice is more problematic for employees with *invisible* disabilities, such as substance abuse, psychiatric disorders, learning disabilities, back injuries, alcoholism, or HIV virus. Many workers, including harassers, do not know what "reasonable treatment" is to these impaired employees because they do not understand their conditions.

Is the employee genuinely disabled or exaggerating?

Resentments form quickly, especially if the disabled employee receives special concessions from the employer for his or her impairment that other workers on the job would love to have but will never enjoy. As the harassers see it, they themselves are not "special" or given special concessions! This makes the disabled worker a magnet for the jealousy of disgruntled colleagues, particularly if he or she is the only one in the company singled out for special treatment.

The manager has a tough time roping in the public voices of these harassers. Their resentment is fueled by the fact that it is virtually impossible to quantify the impact of invisible impairments on job performance. Hence the employer has no uniform standard of fairness to justify the accommodations offered to the disabled.

Unlike cases with many other forms of hostile environment harassment, where the proactive manager has only to deal with a private voice that has gone awry, in the case of the disability harasser, educating the public voice may also be necessary.

But the effective supervisor cannot stop here. As we have noted repeatedly, the public voice is not the whole story. Even if the harasser learns the dos and don'ts of disability harassment, the private voice cannot be ignored. Harassment is always a displaced expression of other conflicts.

The private voice of the disability harasser needs to blame someone for perceived inequities on the job.

The supervisor needs to explore the private perceptions of harassers to discover what is really bothering them about work. Only then can harassers be helped to stop taking their resentments out on disabled victims.

Step 3. Align the Public and Private Voices of the Manager about the Victim

---

Follow These Steps to Accomplish Step 3

To bring greater alignment of your public and private voices about the victim, we recommend that you:

- Explore your public voice. Do you have enough information about the harassed employee's disability to be objective in evaluating his or her needs at work? Have you integrated the employee to the greatest extent possible? Have you educated coworkers on inclusion to prevent coworker resentment?
- Explore your private voice. Do you have strong reactions to the employee's disability? Do you sometimes feel a little like the harasser does about the victim? Be aware that it is common for people to blame the victim in disability harassment. We do this when the harassment makes us very uncomfortable.
- Seek the help of a trusted friend or colleague to talk about these issues, to make sure that you are not blind to some bias that could keep you from helping and supporting the victim.

When managers explore their biases and personal reactions to disabled employees who are being harassed, they are better able to be of help. Getting a second opinion on your perception is good prevention. It benefits you as a supervisor and protects the victim.

Just as the harassers and victims can have problems aligning their public or private voices, so can managers. When this happens, the supervisor cannot protect the disabled employee from the harassment, and the problem escalates. It is therefore particularly important for managers to do a self-assessment for personal "alignment problems" when supervising a harassment victim.

We again start with the public voice. There are a few subtle but common biases that managers harbor below the level of awareness, which, if expressed, predispose the work environment to disability harassment. It is therefore important for supervisors to take a moment and do a self-examination to see if they have biased attitudes.

Managers communicate their beliefs about disabled workers in direct and indirect ways. Enforcing the corporation's antiharassment policy is the most overt measure of the manager's public voice. Does the supervisor regularly review policy with staff, and when appropriate, reinforce its content? Managers are role models for inclusion of the disabled worker into the department. Does the supervisor take active steps to educate coworkers and reduce the isolation of the disabled employee?

The public voice is also gleaned indirectly in the communication between managers themselves and disabled employees. These interactions are more difficult to monitor. It is therefore helpful to alert managers to the subtle ways in which bias can infect the supervision process.

Two common expressions of bias in the public voice of supervisors are *overprotection* and *overvaluation* of the disabled worker.

In the first instance, the disabled employee is excused unnecessarily from certain activities that he or she can perform. This kind of exclusion, though unhelpful, rarely rises to the level of unlawful. The disabled employee can insist on doing the work and the problem ends then and there.

Overvaluing the work performance of the disabled employee is a second form of bias in the manager's public voice. The subtle message to the worker is that less is expected of him or her. The disabled employee is rewarded for doing the ordinary that others do without notice.

Managers should be aware of these subtle biases against employees with impairments that commonly emanate from the public voice, as these biases are hurtful to the self-esteem and morale of disabled workers. While they rarely result in a harassment problem, they can set the stage for trouble by indirectly singling out the disabled employee as being different from the rest.

Misalignment of the manager's private voice can do even more direct damage to disabled employees. Supervisors labor under the same biases, misinformation, and prejudices as other employees. They are not immune to the losses of empathy we described in the beginning of this chapter. One of the more common outcomes is "blaming the victim." When a supervisor falls prey to this way of thinking, he or she is unable to help the harassment victim.

The message is clear. If you supervise a disabled employee who reports hostile work environment harassment, take stock of your public and private voices. They may both need realignment. It is often helpful to talk to someone in the company or to a trusted friend. It may also be necessary to learn firsthand about the disability so that you can clarify your expectations about the employee and be objective in your assessment of his or her interactions with others.

The supervisor has a special task with the disabled victim. Social isolation increases the likelihood of being targeted for *any* type of harassment—and disabled employees experience more of it than most other groups. Just as a supervisor's actions can isolate a disabled employee, modeling inclusion can work the other way. The effective manager seeks to reduce the alienation of the harassed disabled employee.

Step 4. Align the Public and Private Voices of the Manager about the Harasser

Follow These Steps to Accomplish Step 4

To bring greater alignment of your public and private voices about the harasser, we recommend that you:

- Explore your feelings toward the harasser. Are you angered by his or her treatment of the disabled worker? Are you *more* than angered? Are you secretly passing judgment on the harasser's actions without having all the facts?
- Explore your feelings about the victim and ask yourself if you see him or her as helpless? Do negative associations about the disability bias your perception and color your feelings about the harasser?
- Seek the help of a trusted friend or colleague to talk to about these issues, to make sure that you are not blind to some bias that could get in the way of your helping the harasser and preventing future harassment episodes.

When managers take stock of their private voices, they are in a better position to supervise the disability harasser with empathy and impartiality. Because this can be a very difficult task, we advise all managers to get a second opinion on their perceptions. It protects you and the accused.

Just as it is important for managers to do self-examination of their public and private voices when supervising disabled employees who are victims of hostile work environment disability harassment, it is equally important if they are supervising harassers. These employees evoke strong reactions in most ordinary people. Managers needs to understand disability harassers so that they can be empathic and help to realign the harasser's public and private voices.

The problem for the manager is not usually with the public voice. Supervisors are not responsible for making judgments about the harassment incident or about who is at fault. This is the job of human resources or executive management. Managers do not have very much input into the investigation process.

Supervisors are responsible, however, for seeing that the harasser does not continue to be a problem to other workers in the department after a complaint is settled. To be an effective monitor, the manager must be able to sustain a non-judgmental supervisory relationship with this employee. If the manager is *angry* or in *collusion* with the harasser, then the capacity of the manager to be of help is seriously compromised. It therefore behooves the manager to make a self-assessment of the private voice to discover if either of these two reactions is getting in the way.

Hurting the helpless is a universal taboo. From earliest childhood, we are prohibited from aggressing against others who are unable to defend themselves. This taboo has the power of the golden rule, and normal people carry it into adulthood. We have little empathy for bullies, at home or in the workplace.

The matter gets more complicated when the bully's aggression is directed against a disabled person. Psychologically speaking, many people view the disabled as already victimized by their disabilities. Words like *impaired* and *handicapped* communicate a belief system that disabled people are somehow incomplete or damaged.

While we have made great strides in our culture to dispel this myth, it still has a stronghold in the minds of nondisabled workers. Because of awareness training and other reeducational efforts, employees today feel they must hide this belief because it is "socially incorrect." They feel guilty for seeing the disabled through this negative lens of observation. So do managers.

But people cannot easily talk themselves out of the private voice.

When harassment occurs, managers secretly feel the disabled employee has been victimized twice—first by the impairment and then by the harasser. This can invoke a very strong feeling of censure toward the harasser, to whom the manager must respond without judgment.

Depending on the personality of the supervisor, this reaction sometimes surfaces as anger toward the harasser. In other cases, the supervisor's anger flips in the opposite direction, and he or she "agrees" with the harasser's aggression. This is collusion.

To be effective, the manager should not respond in either way. To forge a constructive supervisory relationship, the manager must maintain neutrality toward the harasser. We have asserted that disability harassment is always a cover for other work problems. If managers get mired in their own conflicts about the harassment, they are not free to explore the harasser's private voice and remedy the underlying problem. An opportunity for true prevention is lost.

To circumvent this, it is important for managers to talk to someone they trust about their reactions. Reconciling any inner conflicts will help the supervisor to be more empathic and helpful to the harassment parties and their coworkers, all of whom need the supervisor's protection in the harassment aftermath.

Step 5. Align the Private Voices of the Victim and the Employer

---

Follow These Steps to Accomplish Step 5

To bring greater alignment of the private voices of the victim and the employer, we recommend that, as a manager, you:

- Make sure you follow the company's antiharassment policy and report all known incidents of disability harassment. Under no circumstances is it to anyone's advantage to ignore a victim, especially one whom you also supervise.
- Make sure you follow up with victims who are harassed in your department. While you are not responsible for correcting the disability harassment incident, you are responsible to be on the watch for other manifestations of the harassment problem.
- Make sure you share your observations with your employer. This protects you, the victim, and ultimately the whole company.

When managers fulfill their function as intermediaries and communicate clearly to the victims of disability harassment and to their employer, they are safeguarding the company from further problems.

Supervisors occupy the middle position in the organization. They can either facilitate or bottleneck communication between the disabled employee, who has been harassed, and executive management. If they have successfully accomplished steps 1 and 3, supervisors have listened to the victim's private voice and know what the problems are that fueled the harassment crisis in their department. They have also made sure they are not letting personal biases contaminate the supervisory relationship. What remains is for them to bring the victim to the attention of the employer.

Managers advocate for the disabled victim to remedy the conditions that gave rise to the harassment crisis.

It is hard for some *disabled* employees to advocate for themselves. Unlike members of other protected categories, the disabled are almost always in a class by themselves. They have experiences that are not common to most workers.

It is hard for some *harassed* employees to advocate for themselves. Harassment depletes trust, and victims are in a class by themselves. They are separated from coworkers by experiences that are not common to most workers.

Do these two characterizations of *disabled* employees and *harassed* employees sound alike? They are! The disabled harassed are in double jeopardy. They are twice isolated—first, by their disability and, second, by their harassment. Therefore, the manager has more than the usual obligation to support these workers by bringing the conditions that led to the harassment to the attention of the employer.

Step 6. Align the Private Voices of the Harasser
and the Employer

Follow These Steps to Accomplish Step 6

To bring greater alignment of the private voices of the harasser and the employer, we recommend that, as a manager, you:

- Make sure you follow the company's antiharassment policy and report all known incidents of disability harassment. Under no circumstances is it to anyone's advantage to ignore a harasser, especially one whom you also supervise.
- Make sure you follow up with harassers, especially if you are also their supervisor. While you are not responsible for correcting the disability harassment incident, you are responsible for potential hostility the harasser may display in your department.
- Make sure you share your observations with your employer. This protects you, the other employees in your department, and ultimately the employer.

When managers fulfill their function as intermediaries and communicate clearly to harassers and to their employers, they are safeguarding the company from further problems. Their observations and impressions help employers make decisions about how to handle the disability harasser.

If supervisors have successfully accomplished steps 2 and 4, they have listened to the harasser's private voice and learned what has fueled the harassment crisis. They have done a self-examination to correct for any personal biases that could contaminate the supervisory relationship. The hope is that they have been able to correct some of the issues that led up to the harassment and are monitoring the harasser. As with the victim, it remains for the manager to bring information about the harasser to the employer's attention.

The employer is ultimately responsible for making decisions about the rehabilitation of employees who are accused of disability harassment. Not all harassers can be helped. The manager's honest input is of value to the employer. If a supervisor withholds knowledge, everyone is hurt.

Dialogue between the employer and the supervisor is a "must" for prevention. Human resources is often the intermediary vehicle that connects the two. We strongly encourage supervisors to stay in close touch with HR or another trusted authority in the organization in the harassment aftermath, to keep open a line of communication so that decisions are made using the best and most accurate information on the harasser's perceptions and progress.

Step 7. Provide Employee Training

Employee education to end all forms of hostile work environment should be an important line item on every organization's training budget. But it is especially critical in a company in which harassment has already occurred. In this instance, training is both intervention and prevention.

As we have shown, disability harassment almost always involves misalignment of the public and private voices of the harassment parties and of the company in which the crisis occurred. Training must target all points of misalignment. This means that executive, supervisory, and nonsupervisory employees should participate in a program to promote a change in the organizational culture.

The goals of training are to build a strong public voice that prohibits harassment and to align the private voice to this cultural consensus. The first goal, building the public voice, is especially important in the case of disability harassment. Unlike other areas of discrimination, many employees today still do not know how disability is defined, who is eligible, and what the employer's obligations are. Information can go a long way to dispel resentment and put an end to myth.

But information is not the whole picture. The second goal of training is to enhance coworker empathy. By creating a learning experience in which employees talk openly about their perceptions, we bring the private voice in closer alignment with company policy and the law.

Preventing Religious Harassment

Ezra worked as director of information services for a county government in Iowa. He is an African-American male who describes himself as a "born-again Christian." Over the course of performing his work duties, he frequently recited biblical passages to his coworkers, made public affirmations of his faith and engaged in prayer on the job.

The county determined that Ezra was engaging in religious proselytizing. It further determined that his behavior was creating a coercive atmosphere for his employees and hurt the morale of the department. Ezra was ordered to cease any activities that could be considered to be religious proselytizing or witnessing and to remove all religious articles from his office, including the Bible that occupied a prominent place atop his desk.

Ezra was eventually fired. He filed a charge of religious discrimination under Title VII. In a subsequent court case, the court held that he had been discharged at least in part because of his protected right to religious expression at work.

The Challenge

Religious harassment is the third-fastest-growing type of claim filed before the Equal Employment Opportunity Commission, coming up behind sexual harassment and race discrimination. This coincides with the tremendous upsurge in the expression of religion seen in the country over the past decade in schools, communities, and the workplace.

Religion is expressed in many ways at work. Employees ask

for time off for religious observance. More and more workers are practicing prayer or meditation during lunch hour and breaks. Male employees are growing long beards and wearing yarmulkes, and other workers are wearing head scarves and turbans—all aspects of personal appearance that have religious significance.

The boom in religion in the workplace has brought with it a corresponding increase in litigation. The EEOC currently receives nearly 2,000 complaints annually for religious discrimination and harassment, and the number keeps growing. It is up some 40 percent since 1992. And EEOC statistics represent only a fraction of the real number of cases. Many claims are brought directly against employers in state and local agencies and courts.

Moreover, of the claims filed with the EEOC, fewer cases are resolved today than in the past. A decade ago, nearly one-third of the religious discrimination and harassment cases filed were closed by the agency for administrative reasons, such as complaints that lacked merit. Today, that number has dropped to less than one-fifth. Employees are more aware than ever of their religious rights and are more willing than ever to fight for them.

The corresponding cost to employers has also skyrocketed over this same time period. Monetary benefits paid to employees who have complained of religious harassment and discrimination have doubled in the past decade.

Religious harassment is different from other forms of hostile work environment in a few important ways. First, it is not always apparent where the boundary lies between freedom of religious expression and unlawful religious harassment. We can imagine that Ezra, the born-again manager we described earlier meant no deliberate harm in his proselytizing, though his subordinates apparently felt harassed by his behavior.

Would we come to the same conclusion about this next case of expression of religious beliefs?

John was hired as police chief in a state police department in the Midwest. He claimed he was "sent by God" to save as many people as possible from "damnation." He believed that the po-

lice department was "God's house" and that he ran it by "God's rules."

Jane worked as a radio dispatcher in the same police station. John criticized Jane for her personal life. He publicly accused her of watching pornographic videotapes with male police officers and "engaging in incest and bestiality." He believed that an "evil spirit" had taken over Jane and urged her to attend his church for salvation.

We suspect intuitively that there is a fundamental difference in the motivations of John and Ezra, though there is no "bright-line test" that distinguishes their religious beliefs as more or less valid.

Complicating matters for religious harassment, whom the worker is employed by also makes a difference.

During a coffee break, one employee engages another in a polite discussion of why his faith should be embraced. The other employee disagrees with the first employee's exhortations, but does not ask that the conversation stop.
Should the employer restrict such speech?

In a parking lot, a nonsupervisory employee hands another employee a religious tract while urging her to convert to another religion lest she be condemned to eternal damnation. The proselytizing employee says nothing further and does not make further inquiries about whether his colleague has followed the pamphlet's urging.
Should the employer restrict such speech?

If the employee works for any governmental entity—federal, state, or local—the answer to both these questions is no. These examples are drawn from the *Guidelines on Religious Exercise and Religious Expression in the Federal Workplace,* a document issued by the White House (August 14, 1997). According to the *Guidelines,* government agencies may not regulate the personal religious expression of workers while leaving unregulated other private employee speech, if both forms of content have similar impact on workplace efficiency.

Practically speaking, this means, for example, that since Ezra is a state employee, his freedom of religious expression is protected under the regulation of government standards. However, unlike with the government, these standards do not uniformly apply to the private sector. In nongovernment settings, the private employer *can* restrict employees' expressions of personal religious views in the workplace. Accordingly, the standards for what constitutes freedom of expression differ depending on where the worker is employed.

The Society for Human Resource Management (SHRM) recently surveyed about 750 HR professionals across diverse industries in the United States to learn what private employers are experiencing in religious discrimination and harassment. Surprisingly, most of the employee complaints heard by these respondents were not for discrimination, such as the denial of reasonable accommodation of religious observances, dress codes, or similar tangible expressions of faith.

Most of the problems reported in the SHRM study were employee complaints of hostile work environment, stemming from confusion in the minds of workers about the line between religious expression and religious harassment. Of the companies surveyed, 20 percent reported problems with employees proselytizing, and 14 percent reported employees feeling "harassed by coworker religious expression." Only a few companies reported problems in the tangible expressions of discrimination, such as "complaints about employee dress or appearance" (3 percent) or employees "objecting to job duties" (9 percent).

The SHRM statistics support the EEOC's findings. Religious *discrimination* is less of a problem than religious *harassment*. In light of the rising frequency of these interactions, managers need more than rules to make day-to-day decisions about ambiguous behavior in the workplace.

Manager's Definition of Religious Harassment

Starting with the rule of thumb we apply to all forms of hostile work environment harassment including religious harassment, the harassment *complaint* should not be confused with the harassment *problem*. When hostile environment religious harassment occurs, it is symptomatic of a more pervasive problem with employee respect in the company.

Preventing religious harassment is therefore a matter of discovering where the true problem lies. The important question for the manager is, *who* in the organization is responsible for *what* part of the hostile environment religious harassment?

In most corporations, human resources (or another assigned agent) records, investigates, and corrects religious harassment *complaints*. HR oversees the employer's public voice: its antiharassment policy and complaint procedure.

The private voice is more difficult to monitor. It is what employees really think and feel, sometimes below their level of awareness, but what they express indirectly in their work relationships. The employer has no direct contact with the private voice. It falls to managers to oversee its harmony with the public voice in the day-to-day interactions among the employees they supervise.

The manager's definition of religious harassment is therefore different from that of human resources. The employer has a *procedural* definition, based on compliance to company policy and Title VII. The manager has an *interpersonal* definition of religious harassment. It is based on how employees treat one another. When the two are not in alignment, the risk of an employee incident increases.

Using the manager's definition, two conditions must be met for religious harassment to occur:

1. The public and private voices of the victim are in misalignment.
2. The public and private voices of the harasser are in misalignment.

To prevent religious harassment, therefore, the proactive manager must align the public and private voices of both parties involved in the harassment crisis.

The manager must also bear in mind that religious harassment is unlike other forms of hostile work environment in one important respect. There is no "bright-line test" to distinguish religious expression from religious harassment. The manager walks a line between protecting the victim, the harasser, and also himself or herself.

Manager's Tool Kit

We will give the manager a tool kit to learn how to identify critical misalignments between the public and private voice that leave the company vulnerable to religious harassment. These tools prevent such problems from erupting, or keep an existing problem from growing bigger. If a manager learns of hostile environment religious harassment, we recommend using these seven steps to realign the perceptions of the accuser and the accused in relation to the organization.

Step 1. Align the Public and Private Voices of the Accuser

Follow These Steps to Accomplish Step 1

To bring greater alignment of the public and private voices of the accuser, we recommend that the manager:

- Reassure the accuser that religious harassment is not tolerated in the company.
- Reassure the accuser that religious harassment is one of the ways some coworkers inappropriately express personal hostility and frustration. Coercion is always abusive, even if it is disguised as religious fervor.
- Reassure the accuser that he or she is not alone. Religious practices are private, and all employees are entitled to protection from intrusion at work.

When the manager provides this support, the accuser is less isolated in the harassment experience. He or she can still be angry (why did the manager allow this to go on in the first place?), but setting the boundary between the harasser's freedom of expression and the victim's freedom of choice helps to validate the victim's experience of the harassment. Supervisors must assure the accuser *I am going to try to make this place safe for you.*

In the first stage of religious harassment, the misalignment is between the public and the private voices of the employee accuser. On the surface, we can imagine many different scenarios in which the worker becomes a target of religious harassment. Beneath the surface, however, we will see that victims have more in common than not, in a few important ways.

Starting at the surface, some victims are targeted for harassment because of obvious aspects of physical appearance or behaviors that are based on religious differences. Slurs, pejorative jokes, offensive graffiti, hate mail, and the like still proliferate in some workplaces. Most of these cases today involve victims who are religious minorities on their jobs. No matter what their difference, being the "only one" creates a vulnerability for harassment.

Alternatively, some victims of religious harassment are "ordinary employees" who are subjected to unremitting proselytizing by a coworker or supervisor. In these cases, it is not the religion of the employee that is the cause of the harassment, but the religious fervor of the harasser.

When we look below the surface, however, we discover that these two "victim scenarios" are not so different. In both, the harassed employees believe themselves to be the target of intensifying, unrelenting hostility based on religion. Also, in both contexts, victims often report that they did not know how they got there or how to get out.

This last observation is a red flag to the proactive manager. It means that the victim is thinking one way about the harassing exchanges but feeling another. The victim's public and private voices have come apart. To protect the victim and prevent an escalation of the harasser's hostility, the supervisor must help repair the breach and realign the victim's public and private voices.

Note that it is not the supervisor's job to remedy the religious harassment crisis. Human resources formally investigates the victim's harassment complaint. The manager addresses the conflict between workers that gave rise to the harassment problem.

To begin the process, the manager explores the accuser's public voice. Most victims of religious harassment feel blameless, at least on the surface. In a diverse culture with a long history of religious freedom, Americans have a strong public voice that exhorts religious expression as a fundamental right.

The public voice of the victim follows the rule of "live and let live."

Therefore, when religious harassers forcefully or even aggressively impose their views on a victim, it is an affront to the victim's public voice.

The private voice now has a real tussle, especially if the religious harassment is in the soft form of proselytizing, the most common form of religious harassment reported. The harassment victim is angry with the religious harasser for the perceived coercion. But condemning a fellow coworker for his or her religious beliefs may also rub against the victim's grain.

Two wrongs don't make a right. Wanting to be respectful of others, victims are reluctant to offend the harasser's religion. They do not want to deny the harasser his or her freedom of choice even if they feel this is precisely what the harasser is doing to them.

The private voice of the victim says, "Respect me, too!"

At this moment, the public and private voices of the victim part ways.

The private voice feels attacked by the harasser's insistence. But the public voice still tries to defend the harasser's right to his or her own opinions. The harasser seizes the moment and takes advantage of the victim's hesitation. The victim is trapped in a web of confusion and guilt, the harasser intensifies the pressure, and the harassment crystallizes. By then, it is too late to prevent anything.

It is important for managers who supervise workers who have complained of religious harassment to be sensitive to the dynamics of the private voice. Unless the harassment is clearly derogatory and aggressive, the experience is confusing. When proselytizers package hostility as kindness and aggression as salvation, victims find it hard to fight back.

The victim's public voice says everyone, even the religious harasser, should have freedom of expression. The public voice speaks *too* well for the victim's own good!

Step 2. Align the Public and Private Voices of the Accused

Follow These Steps to Accomplish Step 2

To bring greater alignment of the public and private voices of the accused, we recommend that the manager:

- Explain to the accused that religious harassment is not tolerated in the company. Avoid talking about the actual religious harassment incident or making accusations. Investigating the complaint is the job of human resources. Your goal is to make sure the harasser understands the difference between religious expression and religious harassment.
- Explain to the accused that religious harassment is one of the inappropriate ways that some workers express personal hostility or frustration on the job. Explore with the employee what discontents are fueling the harassment problem.
- Explain how no one's *freedom of expression* is protected unless everyone has *freedom of choice*.

When the manager provides this support, the harasser is indirectly put on notice, and the supervisor shields coworkers from further hostility. Most religious harassers tolerate external control. If you find it difficult to follow this step, pay close attention to steps 3 and 4.

The public and private voices of the accused employee are also in misalignment when hostile environment religious harassment occurs. The situation can get very confusing for religious harassers however, for a few reasons that are unique to this group of problem employees.

Looking first at the public voice, as we have already pointed out, we see that the line between religious expression and religious harassment is not black and white. Harassers, like victims, do not know where the boundary lies. Many proselytizing harassers are convinced they are doing "God's work." Even in cases of coercion, or where a victim is abused solely on the basis of religious status, the harasser justifies the hostility using righteousness as the motivation for the abuse.

The harasser's public voice sanctions the harassment as morally justified.

The proactive manager has to reach beyond the public voice and help the religious harasser understand that his or her religious beliefs are not at issue. Coworker respect is.

The harasser's response to the manager's probe into the public voice is instructive. If he or she is able to acknowledge that the religious harassment violates the right to privacy of the victim, it is a positive sign. It implies that the harasser experiences some inner conflict about the harassment conduct. When this is the case, the manager may be able to get at the harasser's gripes that lie below the surface and that are fueling the harassment crisis.

To complete this process, the supervisor has to gain access to the harasser's private voice. It may be hard to reach, because the religious harasser fools himself or herself into thinking that the harassment conduct is for a good cause. No one can argue with "God's way."

Religion is the perfect foil for hostility. When harassment takes the form of religious expression, it is usually because the employee has trouble admitting to anger or resentment. Shifting the motivation of the harassment from the harasser's shoulders to "religion" relieves the perpetrator of any guilt about the misconduct.

The harasser does not hear the anger in his or her private voice.

But victims (and usually other coworkers who look on) hear it loud and clear. They may not be able to *define* the line between legal and illegal religious expression in words, but they *feel* it. Harassers fool only themselves.

It is not the supervisor's job to change the harasser's private voice. A manager is not a counselor. It is the manager's job, however, to explore with the harasser what the workplace conflicts are that fuel the harassment crisis—and if appropriate, to correct these conditions.

Step 3. Align the Public and Private Voices of the Manager about the Victim

---

Follow These Steps to Accomplish Step 3

To bring greater alignment of your public and private voices about the victim, we recommend that you:

- Explore your public voice. Have you considered where the boundary is between religious expression and religious harassment? If you are unclear, you cannot help the harassment victim define it.
- Explore your private voice. Do you have strong reactions to the harassment victim? Does the harasser threaten you? Do you have hidden prejudice? If the answer is yes, empathy for the victim is limited.
- Seek the help of a trusted friend or colleague to talk about these issues, to make sure that you are not blind to some bias that could keep you from helping and supporting the victim.

When managers explore their personal reactions to the victims of religious harassment, they are better able to be of help. Getting a second opinion on your perception is good prevention. It benefits you as a supervisor, protects the victim, and builds credibility with co-workers.

Just as harassers and victims have difficulty aligning their public or private voices, so can managers. When this happens, the supervisor cannot protect the victim, and the religious harassment escalates. It is therefore particularly important for managers to consider their own thoughts and feelings when supervising employees who are harassed.

We again start with the public voice. Managers may harbor some thoughts or biases about the religious beliefs of the harassment victim that get in the way of effective supervision after religious harassment has been reported. If these thoughts are not socially acceptable, the manager may be uncomfortable admitting to them.

The manager's personal beliefs may be in closer alignment to those of the harasser than those of the victim. Or the supervisor may not see the harasser's behavior as wrong, but as an innocent mistake or even as well intentioned. Alternatively, some supervisors may be sympathetic to the victim's cause but feel generally uncomfortable getting in the middle of any employee dispute, harassment or otherwise.

In each of these hypothetical scenarios, managers become less able to help religious harassment victims. When managers are aware that their personal preferences contradict their supervisory obligations, the managers may try to act as if these factors do not influence perception of the victim in the supervisory process.

We know that when we deny uncomfortable feelings, they only resurface in disguised form. We are wired to trick ourselves. The private voice holds on to all the forbidden thoughts. Empathy dwindles, and the manager is less able to respond in a helpful way to the victim.

It is therefore important for managers to take a self-inventory. Do they have concerns or negative thoughts that prevent them from responding neutrally to the religious harassment victim?

We routinely advise those managers who have supervisory responsibility for religious harassment victims to talk to a trusted person about their feelings. Supervisors need to remind themselves that they are not responsible for settling the harassment conflict. They are only responsible for supporting accusers to reestablish a feeling of security after the harassment has occurred.

To do this, supervisors need to have empathy for harassment victims. They set the pace for the whole department. When they are positive role models, harassment victims feel support and are protected in the department. When they lose empathy, the company risks losing a qualified employee, and coworkers are disappointed to discover that the supervisor's commitment to protect them is only paper-thin.

Step 4. Align the Public and Private Voices of the Manager about the Harasser

Follow These Steps to Accomplish Step 4

To bring greater alignment of your public and private voices about the harasser, we recommend that you:

- Explore your feelings about the harasser. Are you angered by his or her treatment of the victim? Do you also feel controlled by the harasser?
- Explore your feelings about the victim. Do you blame the victim for putting you in the middle? Do you secretly share the harasser's prejudice? How you feel about the victim colors your perception of the harasser.
- Seek the guidance of HR to give you some tips on how to supervise the harasser. Talk to a trusted friend or colleague to make sure you are not blind to some bias that could get in the way of your helping the harasser and preventing future harassment episodes.

When managers take stock of their public and private voices, they are in a better position to effectively supervise religious harassers. Sustaining empathy is important. So is protecting yourself. Accomplishing both tasks can be challenging, so we advise all managers to get a second opinion on their supervision strategies.

If it is important for managers to do a self-examination of their public and private voices when supervising the victims of hostile environment religious harassment, it is still more critical if they are supervising their harassers. This is because the stakes are potentially high for managers in cases of religious harassment.

Supervising a religious harasser is "double jeopardy."

The first challenge to effective supervision is the form of the harassment itself. We have already outlined why religious harassers, unlike others, often have a tremendous resistance to change. They do not accept that their harassment is not "God's work" but "man's aggression against man."

The second challenge to the effective supervision of a religious harasser is the personal liability managers assume in some situations. Empathy drains away very quickly when the supervisor realizes that an angry harasser can turn around and accuse the supervisor of denying the harasser freedom of expression. Managers do not want to be dragged into court in these kinds of disputes.

These challenges add up to the fact that the supervisor's job carries more than the usual risk with the religious harasser. We therefore make these concrete suggestions to managers to protect themselves while also helping the harasser recover.

The first two of these are "Thou shalt nots":

- Do not judge the harasser's beliefs. The supervisor should steer clear of saying yea or nay even if the harasser's belief does not sound a bit like religion to you.
- Do not take sides or discuss the harassment. The incidents are not the supervisor's direct concern, unless you are asked by human resources or the employer to play a specific role in monitoring the harasser.

On the proactive side, the supervisor should:

- Reframe the harassment as an issue of respect. Harassers create hostile environments. Religion is how they do it. Disregard of coworkers is the real problem.
- Help harassers talk about the workplace conflicts that trouble them. Defusing their anger reduces the chance that they will take their aggression out on coworkers as religious harassment.

Because this is a tough job to do, we strongly encourage supervisors to talk to someone in authority in the organization to get concrete advice and guidance on how to accomplish their task. It is also most helpful for supervisors to talk to a trusted friend or colleague to check out their public and private voices, to make sure that they see themselves accurately. It is a disservice to all parties when supervisors ignore their private voices. They lose the most important cues they have to help the harasser recover.

Step 5. Align the Private Voices of the Victim and the Employer

---

Follow These Steps to Accomplish Step 5

To bring greater alignment of the private voices of the victim and the employer, we recommend that, as a manager, you:

- Make sure you follow the company's antiharassment policy. Follow up with the victim, and monitor the department for continuing problems.
- Make sure you share your observations with your employer. This protects you, the victim, and ultimately the whole company.
- Make sure you inform the employer about what the company can do to correct the underlying problem that gave rise to the harassment. See to it that something good comes out of the victim's experience.

When managers fulfill their supervisory responsibilities to victims, they tell the employer what the company can do to correct the harassment problem. This indirectly helps to change the worker's public image from harassment victim to respected employee.

Supervisors occupy the middle position in the organization. They can either facilitate or bottleneck communication between the harassment victim and executive management. If they have successfully accomplished steps 1 and 3, supervisors know what the problems are that fueled the harassment crisis in their department. What remains is for them to bring the lessons learned from the victim's private voice to the attention of the employer.

The proactive supervisor understands that the victim's religious harassment crisis is a red flag for pervasive problems in the department. Depending on what was learned over the course of supervising victims or harassers, the manager should have a pretty good idea of the source of the trouble.

The religious harassment aftermath is a golden opportunity for the proactive manager to obtain the employer's help to make needed changes in the department. The employer is usually upset. No one wants the damage to reputation or the litigation costs that can result from this kind of problem. Our experience as consultants has shown us that employers often agree to training or other interventions more readily after harassment has happened.

By bringing the victim's private voice to the attention of the employer, the manager has a shot at helping the whole department, including the victim. There are benefits to all parties.

For the religious harassment victim, alerting senior management satisfies a need to be heard. Neither the supervisor nor the employer abandoned the victim. This lessens the potential for the victim to become a plaintiff. For coworkers, life in the company actually improves. Positive changes give employees renewed trust in their managers to stand up for them, and in their employer to be responsive to legitimate employee needs.

Something good comes of the bad, making the situation a little bit better for the victim.

Step 6. Align the Private Voices of the Harasser and the Employer

---

Follow These Steps to Accomplish Step 6

To bring greater alignment of the private voices of the harasser and the employer, we recommend that, as a manager, you:

- Make sure you follow the company's antiharassment policy and report all known incidents of religious harassment. Follow up on the harasser. Under no circumstances is it to anyone's advantage to ignore a harasser, especially one whom you also supervise.
- Make sure the accused is in contact with appropriate authority figures in the company who have a commanding presence. This inhibits the harasser's urges and helps protect coworkers.
- Make sure you share your observations with your employer. You are the best source of reliable information on the safety of your department.

When managers fulfill their supervisory responsibilities to harassers, they keep the employer informed so that the company makes good decisions and helps the harasser stay in control. This protects all parties. It also helps to change the public image of the accused from religious harasser to respectful employee.

If supervisors have successfully accomplished steps 2 and 4, they have also listened to the harasser's private voice and learned what has fueled the harassment crisis. The hope is that they have been able to correct some of the issues that led up to the problem and are monitoring the harasser. Though for different reasons, it remains the manager's responsibility to bring information about the harasser to the employer's attention, as with the victim.

The employer is ultimately responsible for making decisions about the rehabilitation of religious harassers. Not all can be helped. Unfortunately, employers usually do not have very much information on which to base this important decision. If a wrong choice is made and the harasser strikes again, the employer is hurt.

It becomes clear why managers who supervise religious harassers should talk to their bosses. The employer needs reliable input from the employees who have the most knowledge of the accused. Preventing a recurrence of the harassment problem depends on a regular dialogue between executive management and the supervisor. Human resources is often the intermediary body that connects the two.

The religious harasser is also helped when the supervisor keeps the employer informed. These harassers understand authority and often have an affinity for strong personalities to keep them in check. Fear of the boss can be a powerful inhibitor of their aggression. From our consulting experiences, we have seen more than a few times that until and unless executive management steps in and acknowledges the religious harassment, it does not stop.

As a bonus, when the employer visibly takes an interest in stopping the harassment, the hostility level in the department also lessens. Coworkers feel protected. They have increased confidence in the employer, and trust in the company is restored.

For the benefit of the harasser, victim, coworker, and employer, we strongly advise supervisors to stay in close touch with HR or other authorities designated by the employer in the harassment aftermath. Since religious harassers tend to respond well to authority figures in the organization, following up with the harasser can help to curb future harassment.

The proactive supervisor is the keeper of the harasser's private voice.

Step 7. Provide Employee Training

Employee training in hostile work environment prevention is important in all organizations. But it is especially critical in a company in which religious harassment has already occurred. In this instance, training is both intervention and prevention.

Training is the final step in aligning the public and private voices of individual workers with one another to form a cultural consensus in the department in relation to the employer's antiharassment policy and the law. Training in religious harassment prevention should target the particular areas of misalignment that stop employees from protecting themselves and stop supervisors from protecting employees, as we have outlined in this chapter.

Starting with misalignments of the public voice, there are some aspects of religious harassment that make it unique. As we have indicated repeatedly, this form of harassment presents complex challenges because of the fuzzy line in the minds of employees between a coworker's right to freely express his or her religious beliefs and religious harassment. In the extreme, we see the effects of this boundary confusion globally, in the form of religious wars and terrorism. The impact of the terrorist's threat on the ordinary citizen is much like that of the religious harasser on the coworker, though of course different in magnitude. Moreover, when world events introduce fear of a particular religious group, scapegoating and religious profiling of coworkers of similar background contribute to more religious harassment on the job.

One goal of training in religious harassment prevention, therefore, is to help employees clarify this boundary confusion. It is helpful to provide employees with a forum in which they can air their perceptions about these ambiguities so that the group forms a cultural consensus. This is at the heart of building a strong public voice. In order to be effective, a company's rules of behavior must be structured around a core belief system that is shared by the group.

Religious harassment also poses a unique training challenge to the private voice. The dynamics of the religious harasser are special in certain ways. In most types of hostile work environment, corrective experiences can help harassers to see their behavior another way. It is harder for religious harassers to shift perspective, however, because they empower their harassment with a moral justification.

The goal of training is to strengthen the private voice by giving employees an opportunity to talk openly about their perceptions of harassers and their victims. Learning to appreciate and respect differences enhances empathy, nature's antidote to aggression in the workplace.

Preventing Age Harassment

AMERICANS ANONYMOUSLY BROADCAST their private voices about age discrimination and harassment on the Internet:

> *I worked at the local University for five years! I loved my job—it was my dream job, finally all of my experience prepared me for this job. . . . I was hired by my former boss. . . . He was transferred . . . and we hired a new Director. . . . My evaluation was written by the old Director and signed off by the new one. . . . I received an above average rating. . . .*
>
> *My new supervisor pulled me into the Director's office and told me I was incompetent! Since then I have received only average ratings. . . . I was very confused and shocked. When I asked "why" I was told I was being defensive.*
>
> *After that, I was treated harshly, different and constantly received memos complaining about something! Everyone in my office was under 30 years of age. . . . Just months before I was targeted, two other older employees were forced to resign! I was subjected to "old age" jokes, lies. . . . new "reviews" were generated for our department but I was the only one who received the review. . . . False statements were made about me in the "review." . . . Others were told I was incompetent, to spy on me and not do things I requested.*
>
> *Before I was fired, they even talked to me about my replacement—who at that time was still a senior in college. They hired him as soon as he graduated.*

How old do you imagine this employee was at the time of this problem? The answer is 42.

Another male IT worker tells us:

I recently hit the midpoint between birthdays, so I am now closer to 43 than 42. While that shouldn't mean anything to you, let me generalize what this means for most people my age: Being 42 (or almost 43) means a lot of things. College graduates are generally half our age—or less. Measured in traditional terms, about half our total work life is behind us. By actuarial charts, more than half our total life is behind us. And in today's world of technology-driven business . . . it means we are working closely—and in growing numbers—with people who are 10, 15, or even 20 years younger than we are. Should this matter? No, it shouldn't. Does it matter? Of course it does. And to someone in his or her 50s, it probably matters a lot more.

What is the truth behind these concerns?

Over the last decade, downsizing, increased use of temporary employees, greater reliance on automation, and less job security have created what some people call a "corporate culture of expendability." This puts the older worker at greatest risk of job loss.

More from the Internet:

By the time you are 40, you have reached the top of your pay scale. If you can be bullied out, the cost of redundancy can be avoided, and you can be replaced with two YECHies (Young Enthusiastic and CHeap) at less than the cost of your salary, who will work insane hours, do anything they are asked. . . . Young recruits will work short-term, and tedious things like annual leave, maternity leave, pension contributions, annual pay raises, union membership and sick pay can be substantially reduced or even avoided.

These concerns are not overreaction. It is projected that the number of workers 55 and older will jump from 16 million in 1996 to 22 million in 2005, and rise even higher with the aging of the baby boomers. The numbers of the unemployed and underemployed will be greater than ever before.

How does the employer react to the growing panic of a graying America?

> *In a survey of 400 corporations reported by the American Association of Retired Persons, "American Business and Older Workers: A Road Map to the 21st Century," personnel directors and company executives rated older workers very highly. But they believe that younger managers "do not really want older employees, no matter how good their skills. So what is the point of sending them an older worker to interview for a job?"*
>
> *Most of the executives surveyed believe that younger workers see older workers as "my mom and dad" and "don't want to boss them." They "know more than we do." Younger managers view older workers as "hard to relate to," "inflexible and unwilling to change," "not part of our generation," and "make us look bad."*
>
> *AARP, 1994*

The Challenge

There is nothing new about rejecting the old, though Americans like to harbor the myth that "back in the good old days" we used to respect our elders. The truth is that age has never been a real number. The *perception* of age depends on the person, and in the case of the workplace, the setting.

Some professions value youth more than others do. For instance, gymnasts "age out" when they are barely adult. At the other extreme, college professors are not in their prime until well into midlife. By law, the president of the United States has to be at least 35 to run for office. CEOs are rarely younger than 50 or older than 65. Football players usually retire from the NFL by age 30, but baseball players go on longer.

There is no "age" in the workplace. The perception of "old" depends on the job.

The psychology of aging complicates the picture for employees still more. In contrast to a *shifting* perception of age in the workplace, our inner experience of self is remarkably *constant* over the entire life span. People do not perceive themselves as different from one stage in life to the next. The psychological self is actually predicated on just the opposite process. Internal consistency provides the continuity of selfhood.

This constancy of self-perception extends even to our inner perception of physical self. Most adults know the experience of momentary surprise when they catch a glimpse of their reflection in the glass without warning. Is that *me?* The physical process of aging is revealed to us only gradually, over time. Mother Nature is kind. We do not perceive the increments of normal aging, only the cumulative results.

This is not to say that people do not grow with experience. It is only to say that self-perception of the fundamentals of "who we are" is constant over the life span. Therefore, there is an inevitable disconnect between self-perception and perception by coworkers as employees grow "old" at work.

Because of this inherent developmental contradiction, we need laws to protect older employees from coworker stigmatization, or *ageism*. Title VII therefore includes age as a protected category. Because it is a psychological and not a physical construct, age has some unique properties compared with other protected classes.

Inclusion under race, gender, religion, or disability, for instance, is less ambiguous. There are "yes-no" characteristics or criteria for inclusion. Age, on the contrary, is continuous. Everyone has it, and at some random point over the employee's "work span," it begins to have psychological meaning. We are deemed "old."

Paradoxically, age is the easiest characteristic to quantify in physical terms but impossible to quantify psychologically. We all have an *exact* age at every moment of our lives. But what this means about our capacity to live and work is almost always based entirely on perception.

Federal law, however, imposes tangible parameters on the concept of age. The Age Discrimination in Employment Act of 1967 (ADEA) prohibits employers from discriminating against workers who are 40 years or older. Some states provide coverage for broader age groups, but 40 is generally the magic number.

ADEA protections apply to both employees and job applicants. It is unlawful to discriminate against a person with respect to any term, condition, or privilege of employment, including but not limited to hiring, firing, promotion, layoff, compensation, benefits, job assignment, and training because of age.

In actual practice, this means that employers cannot post help-wanted advertisements with age restrictions, or use language like "young" or "college student" that otherwise excludes people of certain age categories. Attempts to achieve a younger image through employment decisions are prohibited. Refusing to train older workers on the basis of age is unlawful.

Employee benefits are additionally protected under the Older Worker's Benefit Protection Act of 1990 (OWBPA). This amends the ADEA to specifically prohibit employers from denying benefits to older employees. An employer may reduce benefits based on age only if the cost of providing the reduced benefits to older workers is the same as the cost of providing benefits to younger workers.

The employer also has some protections under the OWBPA. A company can request a worker to waive his or her ADEA rights in certain conditions. The waiver sets out specific standards that assure the employee agrees voluntarily and knowingly to waive his or her ADEA rights in signing a release of claims, and has obtained legal counsel before signing the agreement.

Finally, if an employee requests an ADEA waiver in connection with an exit incentive program, the minimum requirements for a valid release are more extensive. But practically speaking, the waiver permits the employer to plan in advance for the transition of older employees without penalty to either party.

Under federal law, employees cannot be forced involuntarily into retirement or terminated on the basis of age alone. If, on the other hand, an employer can show a bona fide occupational qualification for age-related limits, action can be taken and it is not considered discrimination.

The protections guaranteed by law to older workers are impressive. The problem in translating them to the workplace is that the way in which age, as a protected class, is defined by *law* has no *psychological* reality. A 40-year-old employee is not significantly different in a meaningful way from a 35-year-old employee. The unfolding of time is unique for every worker and for every job description.

These individual differences are lost to stereotyping in a culture of ageism. All older people are lumped together as set in their ways, archaic in their morals, deficient in their skills, and unable to learn new methods. Coworker harassment is one outgrowth of stereotyping, and to the extreme, age discrimination excludes otherwise qualified older employees from work altogether.

Another plaintive voice on the Internet:

I am an administrative/executive secretary with 18 years of experience. I am a Katherine Gibbs graduate and have 55 credits towards an associate degree in Business Administration with a 3.9 average. I am computer literate, detail oriented and personable. I quickly adapt to new environments and learn new software easily. I have held responsible positions both at work and as a volunteer. Since being let go from a position 4 years ago, I have been unable to obtain a permanent position although I am interviewed for almost half the companies I apply to. I have been working through Kelly Services and other temporary agencies, and they are very satisfied with my performance, as are the people I work for.

I AM 54 YEARS OLD!!

While there is a clear distinction between age *discrimination* and age *harassment*, in actual practice they co-occur more regularly than not. This coincidence is more frequent for the age category than for any other type of hostile work environment harassment.

This tells us there is something else that distinguishes age from other kinds of harassment contexts. Its object is to get rid of the victim. In this sense, the harassment is not the end goal in the harasser's mind, as is frequently the case in racial, religious, or sexual harassment. In age harassment, the harasser's hostility is only the *means* to an end.

Why do some employees feel so strong an urge to push the older worker out? Psychologically, a stigma is a defense that is adopted by cultural consensus to reduce a universal fear. Older people tap into the most basic human emotion: fear of death. Most of us just don't like to be reminded of our own mortality.

Manager's Definition of Age Harassment

Starting with the rule of thumb we apply to all forms of hostile work environment harassment including age, the harassment *complaint* should not be confused with the harassment *problem*. When hostile environment age harassment occurs, it is symptomatic of a more pervasive problem with employee respect in the company.

Preventing age harassment is therefore a matter of discovering where the true problem lies. The important question for the manager is, *who* in the organization is responsible for *what* part of the hostile environment age harassment?

In most corporations, human resources (or another assigned agent) records, investigates, and corrects age harassment *complaints*. HR oversees the employer's public voice: its antiharassment policy and complaint procedure.

The private voice is more difficult to monitor. It is what employees really think and feel, sometimes below their level of awareness, but what they express indirectly in their work relationships. The employer has no direct contact with the private voice. It falls to managers to oversee its harmony with the public voice in the day-to-day interactions among the employees they supervise.

The manager's definition of age harassment is therefore different from that of human resources. The employer has a *procedural* definition, based on compliance to policy, and in some cases, the ADEA, OWBPA, and other state and local statutes.

The manager has an *interpersonal* definition of age harassment. It is based on how employees treat one another. When the two are not in alignment, the risk of an employee incident increases.

Using the manager's definition, two conditions must be met for age harassment to occur:

1. The public and private voices of the victim are in misalignment.
2. The public and private voices of the harasser are in misalignment.

To prevent age harassment, therefore, the proactive manager must align the public and private voices of all parties involved in the harassment crisis.

Age harassment is different from other forms of hostile work environment harassment in one important way. To the harasser it is often only the *means* to an end. The goal of the harassment is to make life so difficult for the victim that he or she will quit the job. When this happens, the victim becomes a potential plaintiff in an employment discrimination claim. This is very serious for the employer.

Manager's Tool Kit

We will give the manager a tool kit to learn how to identify critical misalignments between the public and private voice that leave the company vulnerable to age harassment. These tools prevent such problems from erupting, or keep an existing problem from growing bigger. If a manager learns of hostile work environment age harassment, we recommend using these seven steps to realign the perceptions of the accuser and the accused in relation to the organization.

Step 1. Align the Public and Private Voices of the Accuser

Follow These Steps to Accomplish Step 1

To bring greater alignment of the public and private voices of the accuser, we recommend that the manager:

- Reassure the accuser that age harassment is not tolerated in the company.
- Reassure the accuser that age harassment is one of the inappropriate ways some coworkers express their personal fear and hostility. Make sure that the employee knows you value his or her contribution to the company.
- Reassure the accuser that he or she is not alone. You are there to make sure no one in the department receives negative or discriminatory treatment.

When the manager provides this support, the accuser is less isolated in the harassment experience. He or she can still be angry (why did the manager allow this to go on in the first place?), but building a supportive alliance with the victim helps the employee feel valued by the company. Supervisors must assure the accuser *I am going to try to make this place safe for you.*

In the first stage of age harassment, the misalignment is between the public and the private voices of the employee accuser. As in all forms of hostile work environment harassment, this parting of ways opens a door of vulnerability to the harasser.

There is no one profile to fit the employee accuser in age harassment cases. It is most often the case that this worker has no outstanding history of interpersonal problems on past jobs. The harassment is a "first." Because older employees have "been around" for a while, they have had ample opportunity to form expectations about how they should be treated by others at work.

These expectations may be positive or negative, depending on the employee's history. It matters less *what* the employee's expectations are than *that* they have expectations. When these are violated, as in the case of age harassment, it is normal to feel shock.

Not surprisingly, victims of age harassment often report disbelief, even though they intellectually know they are older employees. Remember that we argued earlier that psychologically, self-perception is constant over the life span. We are never psychologically old to ourselves.

Because of this disconnect between the victim's self-perception and the harasser's perception of the victim, victims may not respond right away when the harassment first starts. They may not have the coping mechanisms because harassment is new to them. Unlike the case with sexual, racial, or disability harassment victims, for instance, the age harassment victim is inexperienced in being "old."

This is important for managers to understand. Victims of age discrimination oftentimes do not have the personality defenses to cope with coworker harassment. It is an alienating experience emotionally: First, it is *harassment*, and this is unexpected; and second, it does not feel psychologically valid.

On a practical note, older employees are also threatened economically by age harassment. Paradoxically, they have more work experience than younger employees do but realistically fewer work opportunities. Finding a comparable job to the one they have may be more of a wish than a possibility, especially if the harassment victim is high on the pay scale.

Finally, employees who are harassed because of age are often isolated in their departments. If they had many visible contemporaries, it is less likely the harassment would go on unstopped for very long.

Psychology and the marketplace reality conspire to silence victims.

The victim's public voice is defeated and says, "You'd better not complain."

But the private voice is angry and betrayed. After years of faithful employment, this is no way to be treated. Age harassment feels like undeserved punishment over which the employee has little control. Fears of a shrinking job market close the escape hatch even if the employee wants to leave. Psychologically, we know that prolonged exposure to this kind of perceived helplessness causes depression and loss of self-esteem.

The victim's private voice is deeply disappointed that the company does not care.

The public and private voices split. This is uncomfortable for victims, who are torn between wanting to ignore the harassment and wanting to do something about it. If they listen to the public voice, they will "shut up." If they listen to the private voice, they will "put up." The dilemma is, if they put up or shut up, will it make a difference?

The decision to fight or take flight will depend on the individual's personality.

The proactive manager helps harassed employees explore their public and private voices to learn what is going on below the surface of the harassment complaint. Does the victim feel valued by coworkers? Supervisors have to be especially sensitive to the degree of threat that older workers feel because of the stigmatization by younger coworkers and a discriminatory job market.

Step 2. Align the Public and Private Voices of the Accused

Follow These Steps to Accomplish Step 2

To bring greater alignment of the public and private voices of the accused, we recommend that the manager:

- Explain to the accused that age harassment is not tolerated in the company. Avoid talking about the actual harassment incident or making accusations. Investigating the complaint is the job of human resources. Your goal is to make sure the harasser understands that you value employees strictly for their contribution to the department, not on the basis of personal characteristics.
- Explain to the accused that age harassment is one of the inappropriate ways some workers express personal hostility or frustration on the job. Explore with the employee what discontents are fueling the harassment problem.
- Explain how *no one* in the department is safe unless *everyone* is safe.

When the manager provides this support, the harasser is indirectly put on notice, and the supervisor shields coworkers from further hostility. This informs the harasser that he or she, and not the victim, is isolated if the harassment continues. If you find it difficult to follow this step, pay close attention to steps 3 and 4.

The public and private voices of the accused employee are also in misalignment when hostile work environment age harassment occurs.

Looking first at the public voice, age harassers are usually angry and disgruntled employees who blame their victims for "taking up" work opportunities or employment privileges they feel they deserve. The general bias in our culture against older people well suits the harasser, who is likely to be able to find *some* camaraderie among those equally disgruntled that the victim is not fit for the job.

We have found that age harassment is most prevalent in companies in which the employer, wittingly or not, favors younger employees. This fuels the harasser's belief that the victim does not belong in the company. Inequities in hiring, salary, promotion, and related employment practices that marginalize older workers are a nonverbal green light to age harassers.

The harasser's public voice says that the older employee should move over and give others a chance.

Subtle encouragement by the employer is not a necessary precondition to age harassment, however, nor does it account for the individual dynamics of the harasser. As we have alluded to earlier, powerful psychological reactions also play a role. Older employees inevitably evoke normal feelings about "mom and dad" in younger employees, and, in some workers, these result in hostile or abusive exchanges.

In other cases, these feelings promote positive exchanges between older and younger workers. After all, what is a mentor? This is a work relationship in which we formalize these associations. We encourage senior employees, even recruit them, to bond with junior employees in this nurturing, parental way. This is the best method to transfer valued skills and abilities from one generation of worker to the next. Mentoring takes advantage of the natural way in which younger and older employees interact.

Sometimes, however, the association of the younger employee to the older employee works in the opposite direction. Younger employees can also transfer negative feelings from the past onto the older employee. When this happens, there is a greater risk of a hostile relationship developing. Whether or not it evolves into age harassment will depend on the victim's response, the harasser's personality, and the work roles of the harasser and the victim. But it always "takes two to tango" for hostility to become harassment.

> **To the private voice, the victim is psychologically standing in for someone in the harasser's past.**

The harasser brings something from the past to the present, though he or she may not be aware of doing this. It is not the supervisor's job to *make* the harasser aware. Managers are not therapists and should under no circumstances try to be. On the contrary, managers should take care *not* to talk about the harasser's personal feelings about the victim or the harassment.

It is the supervisor's job to align the public and private voices of the accused employee, however, as they pertain to work. Harassers shift their problems onto the shoulders of their victims, who they believe are the "real problem." The proactive supervisor helps harassers refocus the source of their trouble, take the victim out of the middle, and discover what can be done about the work situation.

Age harassers may or may not ever resolve their negative feelings about the older employee, but they can sometimes be stopped from acting on those feelings at work.

Step 3. Align the Public and Private Voices of the Manager about the Victim

---

Follow These Steps to Accomplish Step 3

To bring greater alignment of your public and private voices about the victim, we recommend that you:

- Explore your public voice. Do you value older workers? Then look around your company. What is the age distribution of the employees? Look at the workplace through the eyes of the victim and use your observations to build empathy as a supervisor.
- Explore your private voice. Do you have strong reactions to the harassed employee? Say the first five words that come into your mind to describe your perception of the victim. These are your associations. Do they get in the way of your neutrality as a supervisor?
- Seek the help of a trusted friend or colleague to talk about these issues, to make sure that you are not blind to some bias that could keep you from helping and supporting the victim.

When managers explore their personal reactions to the victims of age harassment, they are better able to be of help. Getting a second opinion on your perception is good prevention. It benefits you as a supervisor and protects the victim.

Just as harassers and victims have difficulty aligning their public or private voices, so can managers. When this happens, the supervisor cannot protect the victim, and the age harassment escalates. It is therefore particularly important for managers to consider their own thoughts and feelings when supervising older employees who are harassed on the basis of age.

We again start with the public voice. Most managers know the "right thing to do" with age harassment victims. It is not their job to correct the harassment problem, but to help employees feel secure, protected, and, most important, valued in the department.

The private voice is far more problematic for supervisors.

Most obviously, they have strong reactions to older workers, just as harassers do. Age harassment evokes powerful "mom or dad" associations for managers, too, especially if the supervisor is *younger* than the harassed employee is. The pull of parental associations can be quite strong in normal adult managers.

It is interesting to ask why. What is it about age that universally compels these associations in virtually all people? And why do we call it a "pull"?

The first part of the question is easier to answer. Parents or caregivers have the most profound influence on us because they are the earliest and most consistent force that shapes developing personality. Our parents are the "first interpreters" of experience, and the education they give us lays the foundation for how we understand others and ourselves throughout the life span. We first learn how to treat our elders from how we treated our parents.

The second part of the question is less obvious. We used the word *pull* to describe parental associations because our parents' influence tugs away at us most often outside of the zone of our awareness. This is why associations have such a powerful impact on behavior. We do not *see* them, but only *feel* their presence.

Age harassment stirs up particularly strong associations because symbolically it is aggressing against mom or dad. Whatever the quality of the early parent-child relationship, the supervisor is pulled into early parental associations when the symbolic parent—the harassment victim—is hurt at work.

Sometimes the manager of the harassed employee is not a younger worker but is also an older worker, like the victim. When this is the case, the supervisor may find it hard to be objective because of a different pull. Here, the problem is *too much* perceived similarity between the supervisor and subordinate. The manager may find the association too threatening, and either overidentify with the victim or become too harsh. Either way, empathy misses its mark, and the manager is less effective.

We recommend that young or old, when a manager is supervising a victim of age harassment, he or she engage in self-examination. Ask yourself what the pull of the employee is on you? Do you pity or blame the victim? Do you feel protective or annoyed? We also suggest that managers talk to a friend or a person in authority in the organization to get a second opinion.

It is not the supervisor's job to judge the employee or reach a verdict about who is right or wrong in the harassment complaint. That is the job of human resources. It is the manager's job to be an objective supervisor and not allow personal thoughts or feelings to pull in a direction away from empathy for the victim.

Step 4. Align the Public and Private Voices of the Manager about the Harasser

Follow These Steps to Accomplish Step 4

To bring greater alignment of your public and private voices about the harasser, we recommend that you:

- Explore your public voice. What do you think about the way the harasser treats the victim? What were you taught about how to treat your elders? Be aware of biases you may have that color your interactions as a supervisor.
- Explore your private voice. Say the first five words that come into your mind to describe your perception of the harasser. These are your associations. How are they communicated in supervision?
- Seek the guidance of human resources to give you some tips on how to supervise the harasser. Talk to a trusted friend or colleague to make sure you are not blind to some bias that could get in the way of your helping the harasser and preventing future harassment episodes.

When managers take stock of their public and private voices, they are in a better position to effectively supervise age harassers. Sustaining empathy is important. Because this can be difficult, we advise all managers to get a second opinion on their supervision strategies.

If it is important for managers to practice self-examination of their public and private voices when supervising the victims of hostile work environment age harassment, it is just as critical if they are supervising their harassers.

It is our experience that supervising age harassers is not easy for most managers. Difficulties can come from the public and private voices. On the surface, many managers are reluctant to handle harassers in supervision. They do not know the right thing to do and are afraid they will make a mistake and/or get hurt in the process.

Looking first at the public voice, note that employees who harass older workers—especially those who are perceived as vulnerable—break a taboo. Thou shalt not mistreat one's mother or father goes back to biblical times. Like all other people, supervisors come to work with a variety of beliefs originally learned in their families, and later reinforced by their religious institutions and communities, about how parents and elders *should* be treated. These beliefs will influence their attitudes about age harassers, who most often violate these expectations.

The private voice reveals how supervisors may actually treat parents and elders. The private voice too is formed of early experiences, but now not on the values taught over childhood, but on the actual emotional and interpersonal exchanges between parent and child over the formative years. Was the supervisor's aggression tolerated as a child? Or was the supervisor punished for showing anger? The key to how managers react to age harassers is found in their early experiences with significant elders in their past.

The human psyche is complex. It is not necessary for supervisors to know all about their private voice or where in childhood it comes from. But it is advised that they not overlook its power to influence perception. Because harassers of older workers stir up so much feeling, self-examination is critical for managers to identify any personal baggage that might be getting in the way of their impartiality.

Ask yourself, what comes to mind when you think of the harasser? What are your thoughts and feelings? Are you empathic? Neutral? Angry? Withdrawn? How does this affect your management style with the age harasser?

Then check in with a friend or trusted colleague. Get advice from human resources on the procedural aspects of supervising the harasser. Then you will be very clear on your scope and purpose as a manager. However, if managers are not also aware of their private voices, they run the risk of being ruled by them. When this happens, it is impossible to help harassers explore the real source of the harassment problem —themselves.

Step 5. Align the Private Voices of the Victim and the Employer

---

Follow These Steps to Accomplish Step 5

To bring greater alignment of the private voices of victim and employer, we recommend that managers:

- Make sure you follow the company's antiharassment policy. Follow up on the victim, and monitor the department for continuing problems.
- Make sure you share your observations with your employer. This protects you, the victim, and ultimately the whole company.
- Advocate for the victim to the employer to reduce the employee's threat of job loss and future insecurity.

When managers fulfill their supervisory responsibilities to victims, they communicate to the employer what the company can do to correct the age harassment problem. This prevents age harassment from growing into age discrimination.

Supervisors occupy the middle position in the organization. They can either facilitate or bottleneck communication between the harassment victim and executive management. If they have successfully accomplished steps 1 and 3, supervisors know what the problems are that fueled the harassment crisis in their department. What remains is for them to bring the lessons learned from the victim's private voice to the attention of the employer.

The proactive supervisor understands that age harassment is especially serious to the employer. This is because the harasser often has as a goal of pushing the older worker out of the organization. Age harassment is most often coupled with age discrimination. It is rarely an end in itself.

Accordingly, it is very important for the manager of the victim of age harassment to alert the employer of any problems that are uncovered over the course of exploring the public and private voices of the victim. If the harassment incident has uncovered more pervasive problems in the department that affect older workers, the proactive manager makes certain to keep executive management apprised of the situation.

Communicating with executive management also goes a long way to protecting the victim's job. Recall that age harassment victims, unlike many other targets of hostile work environment harassment, fear loss of employment. Whether they are intimidated to the point of quitting or are harassed into being fired, finding another job is daunting to the older worker. He or she may not be able to obtain equal employment opportunity outside the company.

Advocating for the victim to executive management also rebuilds trust in the manager. Other employees will see that you are good for your word. When you protect the victim, you reassure everyone that victimization is not tolerated in your department.

Step 6. Align the Private Voices of the Harasser and the Employer

---

Follow These Steps to Accomplish Step 6

To bring greater alignment of the private voices of harasser and employer, we recommend that managers:

- Make sure you follow the company's antiharassment policy and report all known incidents of age harassment. Follow up with the harasser. Under no circumstances is it to anyone's advantage to ignore a harasser, especially one whom you also supervise.
- Make sure you share your observations of the harasser with your employer. You are the best source of reliable information on the day-to-day atmosphere in your department.
- Make sure you share your suggestions with the employer about what will improve the work environment in the long run. The age harassment incident is only one example of the potentially corrosive effects of ageism on the company.

When managers fulfill their supervisory responsibilities to harassers, they keep the employer informed so that the company makes good decisions about the harasser's continued employment. This protects all parties and helps the company adopt a policy that prohibits ageism.

If supervisors have successfully listened to the harasser's private voice and learned what has fueled the harassment crisis, they know what needs to change in the department to make it a safe place to work for all employees. The hope is that they have been able to correct some of the issues that led up to the problem and are monitoring the harasser. It remains for the manager to bring information about the harasser to the employer's attention.

There are two very good reasons to do this.

First, the employer is ultimately responsible for making decisions about the rehabilitation of age harassers. Not all can be helped. The employer needs input from you, the harasser's manager, because you will have the most reliable and unbiased observations of the day-to-day behavior of this at-risk employee. You have important information that the employer cannot get from anyone else.

Since you have the employer's ear, you also have a second opportunity. Age harassment is a signal that something is amiss in the corporate culture. Though you stumbled into it, supervising the harasser of an older employee thrusts you into an advocacy position. You have seen firsthand the wrenching effect of ageism on your department and how hard it is to mop up the mess in its aftermath.

Accept a leadership role. Tell your boss that enhancing the quality of the work force by embracing diversity is not just the *right* thing to do. It is the only *smart* thing to do. You have already had at least one age harassment outbreak. That is enough of a warning. Continuing to allow ageism to corrode your department could cost the employer millions of dollars in court-imposed fines, punitive damages, and legal fees.

Step 7. Provide Employee Training

Employee training in the prevention of a hostile work environment is important in all organizations. But it is especially critical in a company in which age harassment has already occurred. In this instance, training is both intervention and prevention.

Training is the final step in aligning the public and private voices of individual workers with one another to form a cultural consensus in the department in relation to the employer's antiharassment policy. Training in age harassment prevention should target the particular areas of misalignment that stop employees from protecting themselves and stop supervisors from protecting employees, as we have outlined in this chapter.

Starting with misalignments of the public voice, we have a formidable task before us to completely eradicate age harassment and discrimination. As we have indicated repeatedly, age is a complex psychological dimension that defies explanation. Some people are chronologically young, but "feel old," and others are chronologically old, but "feel young." Despite these utterly human vicissitudes, in the eyes of the law, "old" starts at 40.

Congress first passed the ADEA in 1967, but it took two more decades to expand its scope to its present reach. It is not accidental that the timing coincides with the graying of America by the baby boomers. They are now chronologically "older workers." As the vanguard pushes forward, they are sweeping through the nation's industries and courts in legal battles to fight for their rights.

This is a psychologically and economically costly way to achieve social reform. Thus the first task of training is to build a strong public voice in the company against ageism, just as we have for some of the other protected categories.

The second goal of training is more difficult, and this is to align the private voice with the law. This requires initiating a process to reduce social stigma toward the "old." Stigmas exist for a reason. Unless employees are given a forum to talk about their private perceptions of age harassers and their victims, not much can be done to dispel the fear of our own mortality that lies below the surface.

Alternatively, when an opportunity is given to employees to share their perceptions, empathy is enhanced. Workers reach a consensus on their group's values, and age is reinterpreted as only one of many differences that can be appreciated in a workplace that respects diversity.

Training reduces fear so that the private voice is free to subscribe to and live by the values of the public voice.

Index

About the Authors

Wanda Dobrich, Ph.D., is a developmental psychologist, consultant, and lecturer. She has designed longitudinal research programs for corporations to measure growth in individuals and organizations over time. For over two decades she has consulted to organizations ranging from multinational corporations to small retailers on leadership development, ethics, employee selection, management training, and executive development. She is on the faculty at Rutgers University Center for Continuous Professional Development.

Steven Dranoff, Ph.D., is a psychologist, psychoanalyst, business consultant, and educator. He is a founder, faculty member, and training analyst at one of New Jersey's largest psychoanalytic training institutes, the Contemporary Center for Advanced Psychoanalytic Studies. He is also on the faculty at Rutgers University Center for Continuous Professional Development. For the past 25 years, Dr. Dranoff has been a consultant and advisor to organizations ranging from multinational corporations to small businesses on ways to remove roadblocks and resistances that prevent businesses from growing. He specializes in executive coaching, leadership development, and global ethics, and has been instrumental in the human reengineering of major corporations throughout all phases of the change process.

Dr. Dranoff and Dr. Dobrich are principles of D&D Industrial Consultants, an organizational development firm. They specialize in the area of employment discrimination. D&D designs tests to evaluate employee perceptions of workplace harassment and violence, consults with corporations in the evaluation of harassers and victims, and designs rehabilitation programs for accused harassers. Dr. Dranoff and Dr. Dobrich are expert witnesses, and they advise attorneys who are litigating harassment cases in trial strategy. They have designed a model of corporate training in workplace discrimination. Their programs have been endorsed by Willis—The Risk Practice, a major worldwide insurance broker, and by many insurance underwriters, because of their effectiveness in targeting and addressing the risk factors that lead to workplace harassment and violence. Dr. Dranoff and Dr. Dobrich have established national databases on employee perceptions of workplace harassment and violence at Rutgers University, where they are faculty. They are authors of numerous articles, have appeared on national television programs, and have been written about in newspapers and magazines across the nation for their innovative contributions in these areas.

Gerald L. Maatman, Jr., is a nationally renowned employment lawyer with Baker & McKenzie, the largest law firm in the world, with 61 offices in 35 countries. Mr. Maatman is resident in the firm's Chicago office. He is the chair of Baker & McKenzie's U.S. Compensation & Employment Law Practice Group, and cochair of the firm's Global Labor, Employment & Employee Benefits Practice Group, a group of over 415 attorneys who practice labor law on a worldwide basis.

Mr. Maatman has a primary emphasis in his practice on employment law counseling and the defense of employers and business executives sued in employment-related lawsuits brought in federal and state courts throughout the United States. Mr. Maatman pioneered the process of conducting employment practices audits to assist employers in structuring effective and practical personnel policies and practices. These audits are designed to minimize the incidence of employment-related litigation and to maximize management discretion and workplace productivity. Mr. Maatman's work in this area has been profiled in the *Wall Street Journal* and *Time* magazine.

Mr. Maatman specializes in the defense of corporations sued in employment discrimination class actions. He has also defended hundreds of workplace harassment lawsuits. Among his various cases, Mr. Maatman successfully defended the largest age discrimination class action ever brought in Illinois, as well as the first sexual harassment class action brought by a state attorney general in the United States. He has also defended the governments of France, India, and Spain in lawsuits brought in U.S. courts over their employment of American workers.

He has served as a legal commentator on the Public Broadcasting System, Law.com, and USA Talk Radio, and his commentary has appeared in such publications as the *Wall Street Journal, Business Insurance, USA Today, Fortune,* and *Forbes.*